Hypnosis

A Comprehensive Guide

by

Tad James, MS, PhD

with

Lori Flores & Jack Schober

Crown House Publishing Limited
www.crownhouse.co.uk

First published in the UK by

Crown House Publishing Limited
Crown Buildings
Bancyfelin
Carmarthen
SA33 5ND
Wales
www.crownhouse.co.uk

© Tad James 2000

The right of Tad James to be identified as the author of this work
has been asserted by him in accordance with the Copyright,
Designs and Patents Act 1988.

First published 2000

British Library of Cataloguing-in-Publication Data
A catalogue entry for this book is available
from the British Library.

ISBN 1899836454

Printed and bound in Wales by
WBC Book Manufacturers
Waterton Industrial Estate
Bridgend
Mid Glamorgan

Table of Contents

Foreword

I first met Tad James in May 1993, when I attended his Accelerated NLP Practitioner Certification in Irvine, California. I was presenting NLP sales training programmes at the time and decided it would be useful for me to get a qualification in NLP. However, I was a little dubious about the hypnosis part of the training. "What use would that be to me?", I wondered. Still it was included in the price so I might as well go for it! I went along to the training with my complete knowledge of hypnosis gained from watching stage hypnosis shows on television! I wasn't ready for the shock I got.

The hypnosis segment took place during the last few days of the training. I'd been in trance a few times, experienced arm catalepsy and thought it was a lot of fun. Then, I watched Tad do a demonstration, combining Time Line Therapy® techniques and hypnosis, with a lady who wanted to heal her eyesight. She wore glasses and didn't want to any more. I was transfixed by the elegance and power of the intervention Tad demonstrated. I was sold on hypnosis. Then I noticed something else. During the demonstration I had taken off my glasses. And I haven't worn them since. I've been studying hypnosis and working with Tad from then on.

What distinguishes this book is the depth of study Tad brings to it. Here is a man whose library of hypnosis books rivals the British Library! And he's read them all! That's very important; most people with an NLP background only study the work of Erickson. As you'll learn from this book, Tad has studied the development of hypnosis from its inception possibly thousands of years ago in Egypt and India, through the likes of Mesmer, Bernheim and Braid, to the twentieth century masters Erickson, Estabrooks, and Elman (to whose work this book is predominantly dedicated).

This book also conveys Tad's ability to take complex and diverse concepts and distil them down to their core essence making them simple to learn, understand and use. If this book is your first venture into the world of hypnosis, then it will provide you with a good knowledge of the three main forms of hypnosis, indirect-permissive, direct-authoritarian, and client-centred. This makes the book an excellent introductory text for students just beginning to study the art and science of hypnosis.

If, on the other hand, you are already knowledgeable about hypnosis then you'll enjoy the fact that this book is written on multiple levels. Look below the surface and there are many nuances that will enable you to increase the elegance of your work. Prime examples are the two Ericksonian scripts in Chapter 10. Here you'll find a subtle cross-over between the indirect-permissive style of Erickson and the client-centred approach of Elman. Having used the scripts personally and taught them to hundreds of students, they really work.

Finally, this is a very pragmatic book. It provides the reader with a compendium of theories and techniques that, though never intended to replace hands-on training, gives everything you would need to begin experimenting with and practising hypnosis.

As you'll discover in Chapter 1, the scientific community have recently discovered that the mind-body connection is real. It can be found in the group of chemicals called neurotransmitters. When people begin to realize that the doorway to the mind-body connection is the unconscious mind, then hypnosis will be recognized for the power that it gives everyone over their mind and body. You can start now by reading this book.

Enjoy!

David Shephard

Master Trainer of NLP
Master Trainer of Time Line Therapy®
Instructor of Hypnotherapy
Director of Research and Training, The Performance Partnership
        Limited, London.

Chapter 1

Introduction–The Mind/Body Connection

You are about to delve into the art of hypnosis, surveying the techniques of several masters, from Milton Erickson's indirect, permissive style to the direct, authoritarian style of George Estabrooks. The power of all these techniques lies in the connection that you build with the Unconscious Mind—your own and your client's. The secrets and benefits of hypnosis lie in the trance state, and we will highlight the ability to produce deep trance phenomena. Your ability to move from the state you are in right now to deep trance depends on the rapport you have with your Unconscious Mind. This book focuses on teaching you how to work at deeper levels with your own Unconscious Mind and with the Unconscious Mind of each of your clients.

The Connection Between the Unconscious Mind and the Body

The doorway to success in hypnosis is the Unconscious Mind. Your Unconscious Mind not only holds information that is outside your consciousness, but it also manages sensations and body functions. A moment before reading this sentence, you probably were not aware of the feeling of your feet against the floor, or your back against the chair. You have sensations coming to your body all the time, but you remain unaware of most of them. In addition to managing all these sensations, your Unconscious Mind keeps your heart beating, your blood circulating, your digestion working, and your lymph system operating… and makes your eyes blink without your conscious awareness. It is exciting to know that your Unconscious Mind manages all of that with perfect precision.

A prime concept that we are going to explore is that your Unconscious Mind can communicate with every cell in the body. Until the mid-1980s, people could plausibly say, "Hypnosis is just in your Mind! It's not *real*." But recently, due to the pioneering work of Dr Deepak Chopra, scientists have begun to realize the full extent of the Mind/Body connection. Not only does information from the Mind affect the body, but there is now scientific evidence that your mental processes, mental states, and mental behaviours affect all the cells in your body all the time.

Information is carried within the body in the form of electrical impulses that pass through nerve cells, or *neurons*. Between any two neurons, there is a gap, or *synapse*. In order for impulses to travel along a continuous path of nerve cells, something has to carry the impulses across the gaps. This essential task is performed by neuro-transmitters, which are chemicals that conduct electrical impulses across the synapses between nerve cells.

When neuro-transmitters were first discovered, scientists thought they were found only in the brain. Later, it was discovered that neuro-transmitters actually connect all neurons in the body, forming vast networks of 'electrical circuits'. More recently, quantum physics and quantum biology tell us that neuro-transmitters bathe every cell in the human body. This new knowledge is the key to the Mind/Body connection.

The Unconscious Mind not only manages sensations, movements and body functions, but it also actually sends information that travels to and affects billions of individual cells throughout the body, giving us health or dis-ease according to our Unconscious beliefs. Chopra describes this as your immune system constantly eavesdropping on your internal dialogue.

From the point of view of hypnosis and Neuro-Linguistic Programming, your immune system is also eavesdropping on the pictures that you hold in your head… the sounds that you remember or pay attention to… the feelings that you have… and the concepts that your mind considers. Through the conductivity of the neuro-transmitters that surround all cells, your immune system is constantly affected by the activity of your Unconscious Mind.

There are many things we are conscious of, but the operation—and health—of the body is optimally a function of our Unconscious. Hypnosis allows us to begin reaching the Unconscious Mind and utilizing the Mind/Body connection. This is the beginning of our ability to manifest a number of wonderful things.

What is Real?

In considering the wonders of how the Unconscious Mind works, we continually bump up against the question of What is *real*? This is strictly a question of the Conscious Mind, because at the Unconscious level, nothing is 'real.'

We might also ask, "Is the Unconscious Mind real?" Because the word *real* means 'having substance,' the Unconscious Mind cannot be real! The next big question is, what is 'real' about hypnosis and the connection between the Unconscious Mind and the Body? The answer lies in the fact that the bridge that connects the Body and the Mind is the same bridge that moves us from 'real' to 'unreal.' If the Real is the 'physical,' we must consider the 'unreality' of the Mind. You are now going to be able to enable fluid change in people by knowing that *All* is Mind.

To put it another way, the lesson of the Shaman is that none of the world around us is real. When this statement becomes meaningful for you, you have grasped the 'unreality' of what we call reality. That is a high state of awareness. Zen Buddhists meditate on paradoxical *koans* for tens of years to get to the realization that all reality begins with the perception and intention of the mind.

An understanding of 'the unreality of reality' will assist you in working with hypnosis, because you will realize that the body is just as 'unreal' as anything else. It can be changed very quickly, if not instantly. You can therefore heal your mind and body at any time, relieving yourself of anything from high blood pressure to low metabolism.

Highlighting the question of *what is real*, one of the most intriguing instances on record is the story of a diabetic woman with multiple personalities. When the woman was tested in her diabetic personality, her blood sugar was dangerously high. When she flipped into another personality, which was not diabetic, an attendant drew her blood immediately, and her blood sugar was normal, without enough time passing for her blood to be filtered by the liver and kidneys. The question is, "What is the cause of the diabetes? What is real?"

5

Metaphysically speaking, the mind is one, but since most people don't experience it that way, the division into Conscious and Unconscious Mind is a useful distinction. In spite of some behaviorists' assertion that we do not have an Unconscious Mind, the distinction can allow us to more clearly understand the operation of the mind.

Why do we Want to Learn Hypnosis?

The value of experiencing trance and learning hypnosis lies in attaining power to heal our own bodies and guide clients in healing theirs... power to learn... and power to create changes in our lives.

If you can produce hypnotic phenomena in yourself, such as arm catalepsy (rigidity), major muscle group relaxation, full body catalepsy, or somnambulistic behaviour, then you have the power to produce healing changes in yourself. If you can hallucinate a tennis ball, you can hallucinate a little PAC-man travelling through your body gobbling up cells or substances that have been causing dis-ease. If you had severe muscle pain in your back, think what a relief it would be just to sit down and go into trance, or work with a Hypnotherapist, and say, "Unconscious Mind, go ahead and heal the muscles in my back." If you have clear communication with your Unconscious Mind, you can do that. There is now a groundswell of support for the healing powers of hypnosis from the traditional allopathic medical community.

In addition to healing, the Unconscious Mind opens new doors to learning. If there is something you want to learn easily, you can say to your Unconscious Mind, "Let's learn this," and it will support you. If you are concerned about a presentation you are making, you can say to your Unconscious Mind, "Let's organize all of this to flow easily and effortlessly." Your Unconscious Mind will do all of this for you.

In trance, we can also tap into real power to create changes in our lives, healing what needs to be healed, preserving learnings from the past, and making new neurological connections to manifest our dreams. For these purposes, I teach Time-Line Therapy® to thousands of people each year. If we have rapport with our Unconscious Minds, we will have all the resources we need to create the future of our dreams.

Milton Erickson once said, "Patients are patients because they are out of rapport with their own Unconscious." Hypnotherapy patients are people who have had too much programming—so much outside programming that they have lost touch with their inner selves. People who are in rapport with their Unconscious Minds are also in control of their destiny.

We are exploring hypnosis for two purposes. On the one hand, we are learning how to be superb Hypnotherapists, able to lead others to the rich benefits of trance. On the other hand, we are learning how to be very good hypnotic subjects, so that we can access those benefits by entering trance ourselves.

Chapter 2

A Brief History of Hypnosis

Before we discuss how hypnosis works, I want to give you a short history of hypnosis, so you will have a better appreciation of the art behind the techniques. As early as the 1860s, Pierre Janet, Alfred Binet and Charles Fere began using deep trance to produce hypnotic phenomena. The early experiments succeeded dramatically. For example, hypnosis was used to create a lesion on a subject's hand and then cause it to disappear. These early studies had tremendous implications for healing our own bodies. Since the Unconscious Mind runs the body, hypnosis leads us to amazing possibilities for physical healing.

Hypnosis has been practised for thousands of years. There is evidence in ancient Sanskrit writings of the use of healing trances and healing temples in India. Ancient Egyptian papyrus scrolls tell of the use of sleeping temples and the use of trance inductions for healing.

In the 1500s, Paracelsus, the Swiss medical doctor who discovered the mercury cure for syphilis, was also the first physician known to use magnets for healing. He passed a magnet or lodestone over a person's body to initiate the healing process. People were cured of many diseases by Paracelsus's work with magnets.

In the 1600s, an Irishman named Valentine Greatrakes healed people by laying his hands on them and passing magnets over their bodies. They called Greatrakes 'the Great Irish Stroker' and he was famous for stroking or massaging problems out of the body.

In 1725 a Jesuit priest named Maximilian Hehl was using magnets to heal people. He might have remained unnoticed if it had not been for one of his students, a young medical doctor from Vienna named Franz Anton Mesmer. Mesmer took magnets back to Vienna for use in his practice. In those days, one of the major interventions in medicine was bloodletting. Mesmer would open a patient's vein and let the patient bleed for a while. When the procedure was finished, he would make passes over the cut with a magnet, and the bleeding would stop. One day as Mesmer was bleeding a patient, he reached for one of his magnets and they were nowhere to be found. So he picked up a stick and passed it over the patient's cut and the bleeding stopped! What we would say today in terms of hypnosis is that passing the magnet or stick was simply a non-verbal suggestion causing trance to occur and thus causing the bleeding to stop.

After his early successes, Mesmer made a claim that would later spark a great controversy, saying that it was not the energy of the magnet that caused the bleeding to stop, but the magnetic energy that came from the patient. He called this energy *Animal Magnetism*. The levels of energy transmitted in mesmerism were not detectable by instruments of the time used to measure conventional magnetism, and the name *Animal Magnetism* would eventually discredit Mesmer.

At the height of his fame in Vienna, Mesmer moved to Paris and became a favourite of the French aristocracy. In the late 1700s everyone who was anyone went to Dr Mesmer for one of his magnetic cures. Mesmer became very successful... so much so that the medical community of the time challenged his methods and claimed he was a fraud.

Mesmer then blundered badly by asking the French king for a Board of Inquiry. The Board appointed to investigate whether Animal Magnetism existed included three people notable today: the pioneering chemist Lavoisier; the famous American Benjamin Franklin; and a medical doctor who was an expert in pain control named Guillotin. In writing the majority opinion, Franklin said, "This fellow Mesmer is not flowing anything from his hands that I can see. Therefore, this mesmerism must be a fraud."

Mesmer, thus discredited, left Paris and went back to Vienna to practise mesmerism or Animal Magnetism. From 1795 until 1985, the notion of Energy as a healing art form was left out of mainstream western medicine and psychology.

However, to some extent, mesmerism was still practised. The Marquis de Pusseguyr in France coined the term somnambulist, meaning 'sleepwalker,' which we still use today to describe the deepest state of hypnosis. De Pusseguyr chose that term after he noticed that subjects in a very deep state of trance were, in essence, *somnambulistic*. Dr. Elliottson at London College adopted mesmerism into his practice and was almost expelled from the medical community.

Around 1840, a young surgeon in London named James Braid went to see a demonstration by a mesmerist named La Fontaine. In those days the mesmerist used to stand near the head of the patient and make downward hand passes over the body. What intrigued Braid was that the subject's eyes would remain in an upward locked stare, looking at the mesmerist. Braid realized the importance of the eyes being fixated in causing trance. He coined a new term to describe the fixated state, which was *neuro-hypnosis*. Braid decided that mesmerism did not involve energy transfer. He surmised that mesmerism worked simply because suggestion caused the patient to go into trance.

James Braid wrote the first book on hypnosis in 1843, entitled *Neurypnology*. In that book he clarified that the fixation on a single point or idea is what causes hypnosis to occur. Interestingly, Braid later decided that *hypnosis* was not the right term, and tried to change the name to *monoideaism*, which did not stick any better than *neurypnology*. Thus the name *hypnosis* has survived.

During the same period, James Esdaile, a medical doctor in India, wrote a book entitled *Mesmerism*. Esdaile outlined the use of mesmerism in the process of controlling and getting rid of pain. He developed his techniques before the advent of the anesthetic chloroform that would later be widely used in surgery. Esdaile did over 500 operations, many of which would have been extremely painful without an anesthetic... and found that many patients healed in less than the normal recovery time. Some physicians didn't believe Esdaile's claims and when he came back from India he was almost 'drummed out' of the British Medical Corps for suggesting that one could use mesmerism for pain control.

This debate would have gone on, but chloroform was discovered almost immediately on the heels of Esdaile's return. With that discovery, research on pain control stopped.

In 1864, a doctor named Liebault, in the city of Nancy, France, developed a system of therapy using hypnosis. A medical colleague named Bernheim sent a patient with sciatica to visit Liebault, and the patient was cured almost overnight. Bernheim decided to investigate this strange thing called hypnosis and soon after formed a partnership with Liebault to establish the Nancy School of Hypnosis.

The young Sigmund Freud studied with Liebault and Bernheim at the Nancy School and initially used hypnosis in his practice. In the end, Freud stopped using hypnosis. The reason declared publicly was that a young female patient had jumped up and kissed him. Freud professed to be shocked and concluded that hypnosis was far too volatile to use. The little known history of hypnosis records a different reason why Freud stopped using hypnosis: his cocaine usage had ruined his gums, and his false teeth did not fit well, causing him not to speak well enough to induce trance easily.

In competition with an excellent hypnotist named Breuer, Freud invented 'talking therapy.' Freud said that his talking therapy would not be a therapy for the poor. It would take 100 to 300 hours to effect a cure. His talking therapy became *psychoanalysis*, and this changed the history of European psychology. Freudian psychoanalysis became the rage in psychology and it became inappropriate to use any other techniques. Consequently, hypnosis was eclipsed.

In 1890, just before Freud's rise, William James wrote the first book specifically on psychology, a two-volume work entitled *Principles of Psychology*. This is a 'must read' if you intend to practise hypnosis, Neuro-Linguistic Programming or any other form of intervention with clients.

In the early 20th century, two main schools of psychology developed. On one side, the followers of Freud, along with those of Jung and Adler, who were influenced by Freud, formed an analytical branch of psychology. On the other side were the behaviorists, who reacted against the psychoanalytical processes Freud had introduced.

Behaviorism actually began with a little-known American physician, William Twitmeyer, who noticed that if you tap a patient on the knee with a hammer, the knee jerks. In 1902, Twitmeyer wrote an article for the *Journal of the American Medical Association* called 'The Knee Jerk Reflex'. Included in the second part of his article—and almost overlooked—was an intriguing observation: after conditioning the patient with repeated knee-taps, Twitmeyer would tell the patient that he was going to tap again, but would stop his hammer short of actually tapping the knee. And the knee would still jerk, without being tapped! This is a very early documentation of stimulus-response.

14

The American medical profession may have missed the importance of Twitmeyer's article, but a young Russian researcher named Ivan Pavlov read the article and took notice. Two years later in 1904, Pavlov published his first article on 'Conditioned Reflexes' with the Russian Medical Society, detailing his experiments with dogs. The path of psychology has progressed in mysterious ways.

Research continued on both sides of the Atlantic. At Harvard, Boris Sidis wrote *The Psychology of Suggestion*, which is still a landmark on the topic. In Britain, Milne Bramwell wrote *History of Hypnosis* in 1903. Bramwell described the hypnotic techniques of everyone who had preceded him. This makes his book a useful reference.

The early 20th century did not see further dramatic developments in hypnosis from a medical or psychological standpoint until 1943, when Clark Hull at Yale University published his classic work *Hypnosis and Suggestibility*. This book was one of the first psychological studies on hypnosis. One of Hull's most important observations was that "Anything that assumes trance, causes trance." This is a fundamental principle, which makes anything possible in creating hypnosis. From this point of view, NLP and even visualization are hypnosis.

Many people who practise therapy say, "I don't use trance, I just use progressive relaxation," or " I don't use hypnosis, I just use creative visualization." Clark Hull would probably have said, "Both of these assume trance. Therefore, they cause trance."

Hull is also notable for his influence on the young Milton Erickson, who was present at some of Hull's early researches. Erickson practised hypnosis almost daily from 1920 to 1980, seeing up to 14 clients a day for 60 years. Erickson's profound learnings were to change the face of hypnosis forever. They will figure prominently in this book.

George Estabrooks is another major author whose techniques we will be investigating. Whereas Erickson perfected the indirect/ permissive approach to hypnosis, Estabrooks typified the direct/

authoritarian approach. We will study both approaches, as well as some in between, in order to have access to a continuum that will serve all clients. An indirect/permissive approach will bring success with some clients, and a direct/authoritarian approach with others. Therefore, it will be useful to have both in our repertoire of techniques for inducing trance.

In 1957, André Weitzenhoffer wrote *General Techniques of Hypnotism*, one of the most important books on hypnosis, outside of Erickson's work. Another major figure in hypnotism from the 1950s was Dave Elman. He created a powerful set of rapid induction techniques which offer a different approach than those of Erickson or Estabrooks. We will devote a chapter to Elman's techniques.

Leslie LeCron, in 1964, was also a groundbreaker. LeCron popularized ideomotor finger signals. NLP Practitioners as well as Hypnotherapists use these finger signals as a way of communicating and building rapport with the Unconscious Mind by asking it for answers. We'll discover some of LeCron's ideomotor signals and how they can be used in working with students to improve grades.

Jeffrey Zeig, head of the Erickson Foundation in Phoenix, and Ernest Rossi are two major contemporary writers and researchers on Ericksonian Hypnosis. Zeig and Rossi keep the Ericksonian legacy alive. Their contributions are drawn upon by thousands of psychologists, psychiatrists, and other practitioners throughout the world who use Erickson's indirect/permissive methods as well as Estabrook's direct/authoritarian techniques.

In later chapters, we will examine wonderful therapeutic tools discovered and described by several of the leaders discussed in this short history.

Chapter 3

Trance

Trance and Rapport

The basis for practising the art of hypnosis is an understanding of *trance*. Trance is the state in which hypnosis takes place. It is also a state we frequently enter in the normal course of a day.

My favourite example of trance is on the elevator. You get in the elevator and the doors close, and you look up and watch the numbers flash: one... two... three... four... five... six... You're going to seven.... The elevator stops and the doors open, and you say, "All right... *wait!*... is this seven?" That's trance.

Even more familiar is the driving trance. One time I was driving along a stretch of Canadian four-lane highway from Niagara Falls to Windsor. The road passes through beautiful country with majestic trees and a clear blue sky, and the air is amazingly clear. I was driving and driving and listening to my radio... And all of a sudden my Conscious Mind clicked back into control, and I realized that I was 60 miles beyond my exit! The driving trance is an example of the Unconscious Mind taking over to direct behaviour that would otherwise be conscious.

Probably the most common trance situation of our day is watching television. Have you ever been watching TV while a person you live with was having a full conversation with you... and you turned to that person and said, "What...?" In TV trance, the Unconscious Mind can take in and store long series of images. If you're going to do hypnosis with kids, you can have them remember their favourite TV show—and they'll replay the whole thing for you.

Trance is a normal, wonderful, relaxed, and very *useful* state. People go into it all the time. There are key differences between the trance you go into with a Hypnotherapist and the trance you go into in the elevator, in the car, or in front of the TV. With a Hypnotherapist, you are being *guided* into trance with a distinct beneficial purpose.

A further difference is in the source of the rapport. When you are in a driving trance, you are in rapport with the radio, with the passing scenery, or with yourself. When you are in a TV trance, you are in rapport with the television. But when you are in hypnosis or hypnotherapy, you are in rapport with the person who has assisted you into the trance; and your Unconscious Mind opens itself to receiving information directly and uncritically from that person.

We all go into trance frequently. The issue is whether we are in our own trance without a clear purpose, or whether we have chosen or been assisted into trance for the purpose of learning or therapy. This becomes a major factor for you as a Hypnotherapist when your client is in a trance of his own. When that happens, the client's trance will not 'include' you. In order to work with the client, you must first draw him out of his own trance and then assist him into a trance based on rapport with you. We will explore methods for doing this in later chapters.

Rapport is the basis for success in hypnotherapy. It is the condition in which the client accepts our suggestions unconditionally, without resistance, at the Unconscious level. This enables the client to make the changes he wants to make. Rapport opens the door to trance, the state in which we can talk directly with the client's Unconscious Mind.

Experiencing Trance

As a Hypnotherapist, you will regularly be guiding your clients into trance. Your success in hypnosis will increase as you grow in your own experience of the trance phenomenon. Let your Mind consider that learning how to go into deeper and deeper levels of trance yourself is going to build your effectiveness in assisting others into trance. Milton Erickson would frequently hypnotize his students, as well as having them hypnotize each other.

Many first-time subjects of hypnosis are surprised to find that trance feels normal and natural, and they remain in control during trance. Afterwards, they may have a perception that something 'different' has happened. The event may be a little dimmer in memory, almost like a dream state fairly well remembered.

When a client has remained sharply aware of the process of hypnosis taking place, he is likely to wonder what the difference is between being in trance and not being in trance. In later chapters, we will discuss suggestibility tests that will demonstrate the reality of trance to you and your clients, and deep hypnotic phenomena tests, which will show you your own ability to attain deep levels of trance. The more tests you succeed at, the deeper you can go.

Stage Hypnosis and Hypnotherapy

What about stage hypnosis, where people are asked to do things they would not normally do? Or would they? I have observed that many people who get up on stage to be hypnotized are extroverts who want to be the life of the party. Stage hypnotists use specific processes for selecting their subjects. Typically a good stage hypnotist will select those people who want to be on stage, either to show that they are good hypnotic subjects, or to just have fun in an uninhibited atmosphere where everybody expects them to act silly anyway. I do not believe that the people on stage are made to do *anything* they don't want to. They simply do suggested things under the direction of their Unconscious rather than their Conscious Mind.

In therapeutic contexts, Erickson and other researchers were very clear on the fact that the client has total control. A client under hypnosis will not do anything he would not normally do.

Many of the phenomena produced in stage hypnosis, such as full body catalepsy and amnesia for suggestions, have great value in therapeutic situations. Consider a person with a back problem who is able to attain full body catalepsy during trance. He is able to actualize all his muscles becoming totally tense, then fully relaxed, then completely aligned. Think how this might help in eliminating his problem.

Amnesia for suggestions is often the key to dramatic deeper level results. If your client has a disease that he wants to heal and you do not want his Conscious Mind to get in the way of your healing suggestions, you can give him a post-hypnotic healing suggestion and instructions to forget the suggestion consciously. This will allow the Unconscious Mind to do its inside job without Conscious interference.

This approach can also work with smoking cessation. Simply suggest that the client forget to smoke and consciously forget your instruction. This could enable the client to forget about the behaviour. The *style* differs greatly between stage hypnosis and hypnotherapy. But many useful phenomena are common to both.

A major difference between stage hypnosis and hypnotherapy is that in successful hypnotherapy, the deeper levels of trance are often not required. Erickson observed that we can get results in light trance for some clients, while others need to go into deeper trance for the desired results. It depends on what the client needs. Most of our clients will not need more than light trance to be able to actualize desired changes.

On the other hand, when we can actualize hypnotic phenomena at *all* levels of trance, we are in control of our own Unconscious state, which opens a full range of options to us. A 'runner' whose routine is to run 100 yards a week could hardly claim to be a high performance, all-purpose runner. Similarly, a person who has experienced only light trance cannot gain the full benefits of trance for himself or for his clients. If you have the full range of hypnotic phenomena available in your hypnosis toolbox, you will be able to heal yourself and your clients in powerful ways.

Trance and Learning

You may notice that you are often in trance while reading this book. It is useful to be in trance when you are learning hypnosis. There is no need to be concerned about whether you are missing a number of details at the Conscious level, because your Unconscious is recording everything that you are learning.

Trance is the most important thing we can learn for learning. Because all of our information is stored at the Unconscious level, trance can give us a steady state for recalling information.

In his *Psychobiology of Mind/Body Healing*, Ernest Rossi says, "All learning is dependent upon the state in which you learn." The best state for learning hypnosis—as well as other complex sets of skills—is trance. If you feel that you are missing some details at the Conscious level while reading this book, that is perfect. It is your Unconscious Mind, not your Conscious Mind, that is going to reaccess your learnings, beliefs, and new behaviours. In our Conscious Minds we may think, "I'm brilliant! I'm so logical." But it is our Unconscious that will reproduce and induce trance.

Please enjoy using trance to learn. You will be 'trance-formed' by what I am suggesting.

Now I would like to share a learning technique based on a simple form of eye fixation described 150 years ago by James Braid, the inventor of hypnosis. You can practise this technique now.

> Pick a spot on the wall above eye level that you can gaze at, so that your eyes have to go up. As you do this now, just let your Mind… relax. Notice that in a matter of moments, as you focus on that single spot, you can begin to allow your awareness to expand outward into the periphery. Notice you can begin to see things in the periphery. In fact, you are sharply aware of the things on the left side of your peripheral vision… and now, the things on the right side of your peripheral vision… as you stay focused on that spot.

I call this special state *the Learning State*. It is the first thing that I usually teach students when I want to help them increase their grade point averages. When they focus on a single spot, they go into a trance that allows their Unconscious Minds to soak in all the information the teacher is delivering.

Once you have gotten really good at holding your awareness on that one spot, then you can begin to move your eyes around, keeping your awareness the whole time in the field of your peripheral vision. What I tell students is, "Now you can look at me or the teacher, but keep most of your awareness in the peripheral."

Learning is facilitated by the student's being in a relaxed, receptive, focused state. Here are directions a teacher can follow to guide students in achieving that state.

The Learning State

Ask the student(s) to raise and centre their eyes, as if to look at the space between their eyebrows. They may be looking at a spot on the ceiling or on the front wall near the ceiling. (As an aid, you can tape a large black dot to the wall or ceiling for them to focus on.)

Watch the student(s) for the first signs of relaxation. You will notice certain signs: a slower rate of breathing, relaxed facial muscles, dilated pupils in the eyes. To avoid the chance of eyestrain, limit this eye-raising to two minutes or less.

1.   As you notice relaxation in a student, validate it by saying, "That's right. Very good."

2.   Ask the student(s) to remain relaxed with their Minds relaxed, and to move their eyes down and focus on you (the teacher).

That's the Learning State*. It richly increases the students' ability to absorb and retain what is being taught. There is also some evidence that this technique may synchronize the two hemispheres of the brain.

Most teachers are unfamiliar with hypnosis and will not recognize the learning state when students enter it right in front of them. In fact, if they are paying attention to the students, they may be alarmed at signs of trance. People often say, "We don't want teachers hypnotizing our kids." It might be more productive to train teachers to understand what they are doing when they are hypnotizing the kids, in order to get the maximum learning benefit from the process.

Now we are ready to discuss how you assist a client into trance. Early hypnotists spoke to their subjects in a very direct, authoritarian manner to induce trance. Milton Erickson preferred a permissive, conversational approach which suits many modern clients' sensibilities. He found that he could induce trance indirectly and very effectively using intentionally ambiguous language that caused his client's Unconscious Mind to listen to everything he suggested. The language patterns that Erickson defined are the subject of the next chapter.

---

*Adapted from James Braid, *Neurypnology*, 1843, page 28: "...the eyeballs must be kept focused in the same position, and the Mind riveted to... one idea.

Chapter 4

Milton Model Patterns of
Hypnotic Language

In developing a permissive style of hypnosis, Milton Erickson found that certain language patterns would gain him rapport with the client's Unconscious Mind, without the need for more authoritarian techniques of hypnosis.

Earlier hypnotists usually began by saying, "Uncross your legs, put your feet flat on the floor, put your hands on your thighs, take a deep breath, and close your eyes," *directing* the client into trance.

Erickson developed a completely different approach to hypnosis. Often he would not begin with a specific trance induction, but would simply start a conversation. He would then seamlessly shift into a discussion with the client's Unconscious Mind, talking in a way that would allow the Unconscious to construct the pictures... feelings... sounds... of what he was talking about.

He might say, for example, "I wonder, as you sit here listening to the sound of my voice, can you experience being more relaxed... *now*. As you notice that you're more relaxed, is it easier for you to go into a trance?"

The key to Milton Erickson's hypnotic language patterns is that *ambiguity in any representational system causes trance*. As you begin to think about Ericksonian hypnosis, and how to induce trance, ambiguity is the first and most important tool. If you are used to using language as precisely as possible, intentional ambiguity may seem strange to your Conscious Mind. But the ambiguity in the hypnotic patterns of the Milton Model, which we are about to examine, excites the curiosity of the *Unconscious* Mind and opens a direct channel to dialogue with the Unconscious.

As an introduction to the Milton Model, read—or even better, have someone read aloud to you—the following passage, which is written in hypnotic, highly ambiguous language.

"I know that you are wondering… and it's a good thing to wonder… because… that means… you are learning many things…
and all the things, all the things… that you can learn… provide
you with new thoughts, and new understandings. And you can,
can't you? One can, you know. And it's much more helpful. You
are sitting here, listening to me, looking at me, and that means that
you can learn everything you need now… or you can learn in the
next two days. Do you feel this is something you understand?
Because, last week I was with Richard, who told me about his
training in 1983 in Denver, when he talked to someone who said,
'A chair can have feelings…' You can hear that here."

To see the details of the language patterns at work in this hypnotic
passage, examine the *Milton Model* below.

The MILTON MODEL of Hypnotic Language Patterns

1.	**MIND READ**: Claiming to know the thoughts or feelings of another without specifying the process by which you came to know them. *"I know that you are wondering…"*
2.	**LOST PERFORMATIVE**: Stating a value judgment without specifying whose judgment it is. *"And it's a good thing to wonder…"*
3.	**CAUSE & EFFECT**: Stating or implying that one thing causes another. Stated or implied Cause & Effect patterns include: a. C E (C makes E happen.) b. E because C c. If… then… d. As you… then you… *"Because…"*

4.

4. **COMPLEX EQUIVALENCE**: Equating two things, or saying that their meanings are equivalent.

    "That means..."

5. **PRESUPPOSITION**: Assumption.

    "You are learning many things..."

6. **UNIVERSAL QUANTIFIER**: A set of words that generalizes to 'all' cases or 'no' cases.

    "And all the things, all the things..."

7. **MODAL OPERATOR**: A word such as 'can', 'might', 'should', 'must', or 'ought' which implies possibility or necessity.

    "...that you can learn..."

8. **NOMINALIZATION**: Changing process words (or verbs) into nouns. The most common nominalization is adding -ing to a verb to make a noun.

    "Provide you with new thoughts, and new understandings." (The speaker has changed the process words *think* and *understand* into the nouns *thoughts* and *understandings*.)

9. **UNSPECIFIED PREDICATE**: Omitting the verb, or the object of the verb, or both.

    "...and you can." (Can what?)

10. **TAG QUESTION**: A question added after a statement, designed to dissolve resistance.

    "Can't you?"

11. **LACK OF REFERENTIAL INDEX**: Using a general subject that does not refer to a specific person. Examples: *people, they, it, one, that.*

   "One can, you know..."

12. **COMPARATIVE DELETION (UNSPECIFIED COMPARISON)**: Using comparative words without saying who or what the comparison is being made to.

   "And it's much more useful..."(than what?)

13. **PACING CURRENT EXPERIENCE**: Describing what the client is currently experiencing in a way which is undeniable.

   "You are sitting here, listening to me, looking at me, etc..."

14. **DOUBLE BIND**: An illusion of choice where either choice will lead the listener to do what the speaker is suggesting.

   "You can learn everything you need now... or you can learn in the next two days."

15. **CONVERSATIONAL POSTULATE**: A question to which the response is either "Yes" or "No." In allowing the client to choose his response, this pattern avoids authoritarianism.

   "Do you feel this is something you understand?"

16. **EXTENDED QUOTES**: A series of quotes embedded within one long sentence, where the speaker quotes one person talking about what was said by a second person who was talking about what was said by a third person, etc.

"Last week I was with Richard who told me about his training in 1983 in Denver, when he talked to someone who said..."

17. **SELECTIONAL RESTRICTION VIOLATION:** Attributing consciousness to an inanimate object or a mode of communication to a creature that does not have that mode.

"A chair can have feelings..."

18. **AMBIGUITY**

a. **PHONOLOGICAL**: Using two words with different meanings that sound alike in the same sentence; or using one of them in a context where it could also be taken for the other.

"You can hear that here... "
"You can believe you're unconscious..." (The listener can hear this also as "You can believe your Unconscious.")

b. **SYNTACTIC**: Using a combination of words that has more than one possible meaning.

"They are visiting relatives."

c. **SCOPE**: Using a modifier in a linguistic context where it is unclear which other part(s) of the sentence the modifier refers to.

"Speaking to you as a child..." (Who is the child?)
"The disturbing noises and thoughts..." (Are the thoughts disturbing?)

d. **PUNCTUATION:**

Run-on sentence: Using the last word or phrase in a sentence as the first word or phrase of the next sentence.

*"I want you to notice your **hand me the glass**."*

Pause at unexpected place:

"As you read this… book, you'll learn new techniques."

Incomplete sentence:

"I know that you expect."

19.   **UTILIZATION**: Utilizing all that happens or that the client says.

Client says: *"I'm not sold."*
Response: *"That's right, you're not sold, yet, because you haven't asked the one question that will have you totally and completely sold."*

The next chapter provides a detailed explanation of utilization.

Chapter 5

Utilization

A prime element in modern hypnotherapy is *utilization*. As we discussed in Chapter 4, earlier Hypnotherapists—including Milton Erickson in his early days—would say to people, "Uncross your legs, put your hands on your thighs, take a deep breath, go into a trance."

Eventually Erickson learned by experience to direct trance less and less. He began to allow what would happen to happen. This is called *utilization*.

As you begin practising hypnosis, you can get excellent results in the process of inducing and deepening trance by *utilizing everything that happens*. This means that you pay close attention to the things your client is doing and saying. In response to anything your client does, you can say, *"That's right."* Weave smoothly into your conversation the things the client does and even unexpected things that may happen around you.

I remember working one evening with a client I had led into deep trance. We were sitting very near a grandfather clock with chimes that would reverberate through the whole house. It was almost seven o'clock. As I sat in deep rapport with the client, all of a sudden out of the corner of my ear, I heard the clock make that whirring sound it makes before it chimes. I thought to myself, "Oh no, what am I going to do? The client is in deep trance." As I heard the weight begin to move down on the pulley and the hammer began to pull back, I said, "In a moment, you're going to have a profound revelation of seven ways that you know that you've changed." And the hammer came down and sounded a profound *Bongg!*, and I said, "…one." *Bongg!* "…two." *Bongg!* "…three." *Bongg!* So utilize, utilize, utilize. Use everything that happens in the context of hypnosis to deepen the client's trance. When my clock client came out of trance, she said it had been one of the most profound experiences of her life.

Erickson was a master at utilization. He would use everything that occurred in trance. He would say to the client, "I'm not sure if you've noticed this, but your breathing has slowed down. And your eyes have become fixated on that spot on the wall. And whether or not you've noticed this, perhaps one or the other of your arms has become slightly stiff." Erickson would utilize everything that happened because he loved *paying attention* to things.

You can utilize everything that happens in the context of a client's trance. For example, if you see something that the client is about to do, tell the client to do it. And when they do it, simply say, "That's right." That's utilization.

Let us suppose that you say to your client, "In a moment you're going to blink." (That is an automatic thing that will happen whether you talk about it or not.) After a long or a short moment, the client will blink, and you say, "That's right!" When the client blinks, their Unconscious Mind begins to accept the idea that it triggered the blink in response to your suggestion. And in accepting the suggestion to blink, the client's Unconscious becomes more accepting to additional suggestions. Utilization is powerful.

The focus on paying attention to even tiny things that the client does is very important. Psychoanalysis attempted to do away with this. The psychoanalyst would sit at the head of the couch with the patient facing away from him, and neither would see the other. Erickson initially came under a great deal of criticism for suggesting that the therapist look at the client and observe certain things. And this practice added greatly to his effectiveness.

So I suggest that you look at your clients while you're working with them in hypnosis. It is a good idea to have your chair at a 90 to 135 degree angle to the client's chair, for two reasons. First, this angle will enable you to take full advantage of peripheral vision, noticing anything from the events in the room to the rise and fall of the client's chest as they breathe. Second, this angle will enable the client to have space—avoiding any feelings of invasion—and feel safe; this will strengthen your rapport with the client. And *you will be paying attention* to the client.

A special variety of utilization is the use of convincers to build the client's belief in the reality of trance. People often expect trance to be something remarkably different from anything they have experienced. They may discount the level of trance that they attain because it feels so familiar. As often as I tell my clients, "Trance is a normal state. It's going to feel very familiar," they sometimes have doubts about whether anything is really happening.

A convincer has the purpose of showing the client that they are or have been in trance. The best convincer is the client's own behaviour, preferably an action or behaviour in which there is some dissonance between the Conscious Mind and the Unconscious Mind. For example, when a client has arm catalepsy, you can have them open their eyes and look at their rigid, raised arm. When you then ask the client, "Are you in trance?" they have a solid convincer.

Likewise, you can notice certain things clients are about to do even before they become aware of them. You can ask them to do those things, and as they act, apparently in response to your suggestion, and you say, "That's right," their own behaviour becomes a convincer that they are following your suggestions.

Our emphasis on utilization stems from Erickson's discoveries of its great power. But utilization works equally well with the techniques of the other masters whose work we will discuss. The following exercise will allow you to experience the naturalness and the effectiveness of utilization. Do it with a partner who shares your interest in hypnosis.

Utilization Exercise for Two People

One person will act as the Hypnotherapist, the other as the Client. The Hypnotherapist sits across from the Client at a comfortable 130-degree angle, and goes into rapport with the Client. From an NLP point of view, this means matching the Client's physiology: sit the same way the Client is sitting; match the Client's head tilt, breathing, posture, even the angle of their spine. As you do this, Hypnotherapist, go into a trance.

If you are in rapport with the Client, and you are in a trance, then the Client will go into a trance too. Every time you notice that the Client is doing anything that looks like going into a trance, utilize what you see by saying, *"That's right."* You will only use two words during this entire trance induction: *"That's right."*

Client, notice how somebody saying *"That's right"* to you when you produce trance behaviour amplifies your trance.

After 5 minutes, reverse roles, so that each of you has experienced utilization both as the Hypnotherapist and the Client.

Chapter 6

Personal History

Questioning Techniques

At the beginning of your first session with a new client, you need to gather detailed information about events in the client's life leading up to his reasons for seeking your help. Ask questions based on the client's *presenting problem* and questions about what they want to change. The time you spend asking questions is an excellent time to establish rapport.

I recommend the set of questions below, which will lead you to the client's presenting problem and its root cause. As you ask the questions, observe whether the answers suggest that the client is *at cause* or *at effect* in the events that shape his life. In other words, does the client perceive that they are in control of the direction their life is taking, or that outside forces determine what happens to them?

Questions for Obtaining Detailed Personal History

1. **Why are you here? Why else? Why else?**
   Elicit all of the reasons the client has come to see you.

2. **How do you know you have this problem?**
   Elicit the client's strategy for having the problem and any diagnoses made.

3. **How long have you had the problem?**
   Was there a time when you didn't have it?
   What have you done about it?

4. **What happened the first time you had the problem?**
   What emotions were present?

5. **What events have happened since then?**
   What emotions were present?

6. **In each of these events, what is the relationship between the event and your current situation in life?**

---

7. **Tell me about your parents, brothers, sisters, and so on.** What is the relationship between this person (each one) and your current situation?

8. **Tell me about your childhood in relationship to this problem.**

9. **Is there a purpose for having this problem?** Ask your Unconscious Mind.

10. **When did you choose to have this situation created?** Why? Ask your Unconscious Mind.

11. **Is there something your Unconscious Mind wants you to know**, or is there something you're not getting which, if you got it, would allow the problem to disappear?

12. **Is it OK with your Unconscious Mind to support us in removing this problem today,** and to allow you to have an undeniable experience of the problem disappearing, when we have completed the session?

This set of questions is designed to draw answers from the client that will clearly show you what interventions during hypnosis will be the most useful. Pay attention to everything the client tells you. As you take notes, keep in mind that *every presenting problem is an example of something*. To identify higher level presenting problems that the client is not consciously aware of, you can ask, "What is this an example of?" To get more detail on the effects of a major presenting problem, ask, "Can you give me an example of that?" In this way, you will be moving up and down a hierarchy of issues structured like this:

GREATER PROBLEM				
Presenting Problem			Presenting Problem	
Example	Example	Example	Example	Example

Time-Line Therapy® Master Practitioner Training provides excellent practice in obtaining a detailed personal history. Another good source is Dr A.M. Krasner's book *The Wizard Within*, where he outlines a way of asking the client very specific questions about the presenting problem. If you have learned NLP, you can use the questions that are "The Keys To An Achievable Outcome." As a Hypnotherapist, you need to get a clear idea of the presenting problem and what intervention is likely to help the client in resolving it. For this purpose, the personal history is your best tool.

Using the Meta Model

As the client answers your questions on their personal history, they will frequently generalize, distort information (usually unintentionally), and leave out details. You can elicit the detailed information you need by using the **Meta Model**, an NLP system of language patterns and clarifying questions. The patterns are common language changes that 'hide' information the speaker does not want to acknowledge or communicate, either consciously or unconsciously. The questions are designed to recover the hidden information. The Meta Model is mapped on the following pages.

Response	Prediction	Pattern
DISTORTIONS		
1. Mind Reading: Claiming to know someone's internal state, e.g.: "You don't like me."	"How do you know I don't like you?"	Recovers source of the information.
2. Lost Performative: Value judgments where the person doing the judging is left out, e.g.: "It's bad to be inconsistent."	"Who says it's bad?" "According to whom?" "How do you know it's bad?"	Gathers evidence. Recovers source of belief, the Performative, or the strategy for the belief.
3. Cause—Effect: Where cause is wrongly put outside the self, e.g.: "You make me sad."	"How does what I'm doing cause you to choose to feel sad?" "How, specifically?"	Recovers the choice.
4. Complex Equivalence: Where two experiences are interpreted as being synonymous, e.g.: "She's always yelling at me, she doesn't like me."	"How does her yelling mean that she doesn't...?" "Have you ever yelled at someone you liked?"	Recovers Complex Equivalence or counter example.
5. Presuppositions, e.g.: "If my husband knew how much I suffered, he wouldn't do that." There are 3 Presuppositions in this sentence: (1) I suffer, (2) My husband acts in some way, and (3) My husband doesn't know I suffer.	(1) "How do you choose to suffer?" (2) "How is he (re)acting?" (3) "How do you know he doesn't know?"	Specifies the choice and the verb and what he does. Recovers the Internal Representation and the Complex Equivalence.
GENERALIZATIONS		
6. Universal Quantifiers: Universal Generalizations such as 'all', 'every', 'never', 'everyone', 'no one', etc, e.g.: "She never listens to me."	Find Counter Examples. "Never?" "What would happen if she did?"	Recovers Counter Examples, Effects, Outcomes.

7. Modal Operators:

a. Modal Operators of Necessity, such as 'should', 'shouldn't', 'must', 'must not', 'have to', 'need to', 'it is necessary', e.g.: "I have to take care of her."

a. "What would happen if you didn't?" ("What would happen if you did?") Also, "Or?"

Recovers Effects, Outcome.

b. Modal Operators of Possibility (or Impossibility), such as 'can' / 'can't', 'will' / 'won't', 'may' / 'may not', 'possible' / 'impossible', e.g.: "I can't tell him the truth."

b. "What prevents you?" ("What would happen if you did?")

Recovers Causes.

DELETIONS

8. Nominalizations: Process words which have been frozen in time, making them nouns, e.g.: "There is no communication here."

"Who's not communicating what to whom?" "How would you like to communicate?"

Turns it back into a process, recovers deletion and reference.

9. Unspecified Verbs, e.g.: "He rejected me."

"How, specifically?"

Specifies the verb.

10. Simple Deletions:

a. Of person or thing, e.g.: "I am uncomfortable."

a. "About what / whom?"

a. Recovers Deletion.

b. Lack of Referential Index: Fails to specify a person or thing, e.g.: "They don't listen to me."

b. "Who, specifically, doesn't listen to you?"

b. Recovers Referential Index.

c. Comparative Deletions: As in good, better, best, worst, more, less, most, least, e.g.: "She's a better person."

c. "Better than whom?" "Better at what?" "Compared to whom, what?"

c. Recovers Comparative Deletion.

In examining the Meta Model, you probably noticed that all ten categories also occur in the Milton Model (Chapter 4). Both models summarize language patterns that delete, distort and generalize information. The two models have exactly opposite purposes.

As a Hypnotherapist, you can use the Meta Model to get your client to supply specific details they have omitted. The omissions may be unintentional, but commonly involve details that the client is not comfortable acknowledging. These details will show you why the client is there for help.

The purpose of the Milton Model is for the Hypnotherapist to omit details and speak with deliberate vagueness that will engage the interest of the client's Unconscious Mind and allow it to supply withheld or forgotten details from the client's experience.

There is a further contrast between the two models that is a key to success in hypnotism. As we discussed in Chapter 3, the client may come to you in a trance of their own, which does not 'include' you. Questions from the Meta Model focus the client's attention on details; this concentration on details will draw them *out* of trance. Once you have obtained the personal history, you can then use Milton Model language patterns to lead the client into a *new* trance built on rapport with you, the Hypnotherapist. It is in this trance that you and the client will accomplish your work.

Chapter 7

Pre-Talk and Suggestibility Tests

The success of a hypnosis session often rests on the effectiveness of the Pre-talk, the conversation you have with the client before actually inducing trance. You and the client will get the best results from the session if the client feels comfortable about the process of hypnosis, excited about its potential benefits, and convinced that it will work.

Addressing Misconceptions

During the Pre-talk, you can allay any fears or misconceptions the client may have about hypnosis. The most common misconception is that the client expects to be 'out' to the point where they will have no memory of the experience. That does not happen unless you give a specific suggestion to forget.

A light trance will likely feel no different from relaxation. Since trance is a normal, natural state, clients will have a feeling of familiarity no matter how deep in trance they go. Tell your clients, "Don't expect to 'feel' hypnotized. Trance is not about being zonked out. It's a normal, natural state. But do expect to feel very relaxed." It is sometimes useful to point out common examples of trance from the client's everyday experience, such as the driving trance.

A more serious concern for some clients is based on the misconception that somehow the client is giving over *control* to the Hypnotherapist. Hypnosis is not power over another person, but rather a complex interaction between Hypnotherapist and client. It is a cooperative act. As you did the Utilization Exercise in the previous chapter, you probably noticed that most of the exercise was a process of becoming synchronized with your partner. Whether or not you were aware of it, the two of you were sending waves of energy toward each other, synchronizing and coming together, like a dance. Think of hypnosis as two people cooperating toward a mutual end, which is to establish better communication with the Unconscious Mind.

Make sure your clients understand that *they* are in control: all hypnosis is self-hypnosis. This is an important concept for you—and your client—to understand. Hypnosis is something that the client will do with himself, for himself. If a client says, "You can't hypnotize me!" he is right. He is the only person who can hypnotize himself. He is the only one who moves himself into trance. You as Hypnotherapist are a facilitator or guide. Since all hypnosis is self-hypnosis, the client is always in control.

Clients accept only the suggestions that are consistent with their values and beliefs. A client cannot be made to do something in hypnosis that they would not normally do. And a client will not follow a post-hypnotic suggestion to do something in conflict with their values and beliefs.

In the Pre-talk, I often tell a client, "During hypnosis, you need to know that you are in control. If I ask you to stand up, you will probably do it. But if I told you to go rob a bank, you would not do that... unless that was your mode of operation in the waking state." If the control issue has been very much on the client's mind, I say, "At every moment during hypnosis, you're in control. In fact, you will notice when we reach the deeper stages of hypnosis, they are set up so at any given moment you can say, 'No, I don't want to do that.'"

Another occasional concern is that of the client who asks, "What happens if I get stuck in trance?" My response is, "Pray for it!" People in Zen monasteries meditate for years, pursuing deeper and longer trances until they have a moment of enlightenment and become 'The Buddha.'

Actually, a client you assist into trance will not get stuck; you can readily lead them out at any time. In fact, if the client stays conscious during trance, he can bring himself out.

I can easily put myself into deep trance... and sometimes fall asleep. When this happens, I have a wonderful deep sleep and wake up at the end of it. You can do deep trance with yourself. You can either set an alarm to ensure against overtrancing, or choose to just fall asleep and have a nice nap. Whatever way you choose to go into a deep trance of self-hypnosis is the perfect way for you.

Helping the Client Understand Trance and its Benefits

The more your client understands about the trance state, the better they can play their role in the cooperative interaction that helps them achieve trance. Once you have observed the level of their curiosity and interest, it may be useful to briefly explain hypnosis in terms of the Mind/Body connection and the healing possibilities that are made possible by opening up communication with the Unconscious Mind. The client can play their role best if they understand that rapport with you will 'open the door' to rapport with their own Unconscious Mind.

Critical to success in therapy are the client's confidence and trust in the Hypnotherapist. You can establish trust best by asking questions to get a clear understanding of what the client wants to gain through your guidance. Questions about the client's intent will show your support more clearly than any statements you can make.

Suggestibility Tests

When the client is comfortable, even excited, about the idea of experiencing trance, there is one more very useful step before you induce trance: suggestibility tests. Keep in mind that everyone is suggestible to some degree.

The main purpose of suggestibility tests is to convince *a client* that they are suggestible. The client needs to know clearly that they are *indeed* suggestible and can respond to hypnosis. Before I begin a suggestibility test, I usually say, "You know, my mother was told by her mother, 'Do not be suggestible!' In fact many people in previous generations thought that being suggestible was not good. But if you want to attain the healthiest state, and if you want to have good communication with your Unconscious Mind, then you need to learn how to let your Mind give suggestions to your body. Thus it is very useful to be suggestible. If you get good at being suggestible, you will be able, at will, to tell your Unconscious Mind to do anything you want... and it will do it for you."

Suggestibility Test Exercises for Two People

Here are three suggestibility tests for you to try out now with a partner, and to use later as needed for convincing a client of their own suggestibility.

First is the **Dictionary and Balloon Test**.

Dictionary and Balloon Test

Find a place where you and your partner have room to move around. The Hypnotherapist says to the client,

"Hold both of your arms stretched out in front of you, with the palms of your hands down, at shoulder height. Close your eyes. Now turn your right hand over so it is facing palm up.

"Now, I'd like you to imagine a *heavy* book—maybe Webster's Unabridged Dictionary—in your right hand. Imagine it is so heavy that it's pulling your whole right arm down... *down... DOWN*. Now imagine tied to your left wrist a big blue balloon, filled with lots of helium, lifting... *lifting... LIFTING...* your left hand upward... *upward... UPWARD*. A big blue balloon, lifting your left hand upward, *upward...* And a heavy dictionary getting heavier and HEAVIER.... And a big blue balloon lifting, lifting, and LIFTING.... And the dictionary getting *heavier* and *HEAVIER*.... (Continue as needed.) Now, open your eyes, and look at your hands!

"If your arms moved from being parallel, then you are suggestible, and your Body will listen to suggestions from your Mind. Whatever results you achieved, please consider this question: 'What do you think the total effect of all the suggestions your Mind gives your Body has been over the last 30 years?' This exercise lasts from 10 to 30 seconds. Over a 30-year time frame, what is the net effect of all the suggestions you are giving yourself unconsciously?"

Our second suggestibility test is the **Finger Vice Test**. You and your partner can do this sitting down.

Finger Vice Test

The Hypnotherapist says to the client, "Clasp your hands together in front of you with fingers interlocked, and raise your two forefingers straight upward. Move your forefingers an inch apart and freeze them in that position, making sure to clasp your hands nice and tight with your other fingers.

"Now I want you to imagine a little vice or clamp around your forefingers. I'm going to turn the little lever and I want you to notice what happens as the vice starts to close." (Make a turning motion with your hand.) "Look how your fingers are starting to move together." Continue this way until the client's forefingers are pressed against each other.

You can also repeat the test without actually making the turning motion. The Hypnotherapist says, "Pull your forefingers apart and imagine the vice again. Squeezing your hands nice and tight and trying to hold your forefingers apart, imagine the little lever on the vice turning and turning and bringing your forefingers together. Look how your forefingers are coming together."

What is fun about this is that the client gets to see a second-by-second demonstration of the effect of their imagination on their fingers.

You may occasionally have a client who will 'mismatch'. Their fingers will stay apart even as they imagine the vice. A Mismatcher is someone who habitually contradicts statements and suggestions. If you say, "It's a great day," they will reply, "No, it's awful." If you say, "This is a terrible restaurant," they will say, "It's not so bad."

Mismatchers are easy to deal with. You can tell them to do the opposite of what you really want them to do. The Finger Vice Test is a good way to find out if your client is a Mismatcher. If their fingers stay apart or go further apart as you have them imagine the clamp, change your approach. You can say, "Even though the vice is closing, don't let your fingers move toward each other yet." If you give a Mismatcher properly contrary cues, their Unconscious Mind will at some point move the fingers together. When you are later inducing trance, you can say, "Don't go into a trance yet. Don't fall deeply asleep. Don't accept these suggestions totally and completely as you listen carefully to the sound of my voice."

Remember that the purpose of suggestibility tests is to convince the client that they can be suggestible and go into hypnosis. There is no need to convince you, because you already know that every-one is suggestible to some degree.

Our third suggestibility test is the **Postural Sway**.

The Postural Sway

Find a place where the client can stand in an upright 'mil-itary' position. The Hypnotherapist says to the client, "Close your eyes and turn your face up toward the ceil-ing, with your eyes closed. Imagine that you are swaying back and forth. Safely of course, back and forth... back and forth... back and forth. Notice that you are actually beginning to sway, safely of course. Your Unconscious Mind will always catch you... back and forth... (If you are not swaying, it may be because your face isn't turned fully up toward the ceiling) ... back and forth. Now come on back and open your eyes."

Suggestibility Tests as Convincers

These three simple, standard suggestibility tests are designed to allow a client who has never been in trance before to experience their own suggestibility. They act as convincers. I recommend doing at least one of these tests before you hypnotize the client the first time.

I usually do all three, saying, "You may be better at one than the others. We are using different muscle groups and different parts of the body." In the Dictionary and Balloon Test, we use the full arm and shoulder muscle group. In the Finger Vice, we use the hands. In the Postural Sway, we use the legs. Different muscle groups may be suggestible at different levels for a person, so I do all three tests to give the client an opportunity to see which one they do best. This gives me information about which muscle group is most suggestible.

Suggestibility tests are not particularly Ericksonian; they come from standard hypnotherapy. We find that almost everyone will respond to at least one of the tests. Before doing the tests, you need to tell the client, "The reason it's good to be suggestible is that you'll be able to have your Mind make suggestions to your Body at will, and you'll be able to heal anything." If you have this discussion first, you will have a very high success rate in suggestibility tests and the hypnosis that follows.

Some people walk into a Hypnotherapy session determined to say "I never felt hypnotized" when they leave. In other cases, because the hypnotic state is so natural, less skeptical people may say afterwards, "I don't think I was hypnotized. I just felt relaxed and comfortable." With clients of both types, suggestibility tests act as powerful pre-trance convincers.

If for some reason the suggestibility tests do not work, this does not mean that the client will not go into trance. They may tell you that they are not hypnotized, that they feel nothing different from normal. Neither the client, nor you, may have any idea that they are in trance, and the next moment their arm may be suspended in mid-air.

Students often ask if there is any relationship between the suggestibility tests and the depth of hypnosis a person is able to reach. I avoid predicting depth of trance from the suggestibility tests because my pre-judgment might keep the client from going as deep as they might. I use the suggestibility tests solely as a means of convincing the client that they are hypnotizable.

Chapter 8

Stages of Hypnosis

Recognizing Levels of Trance

To ensure that the client has the most successful hypnotic experience, it is important that you continually recognize what level of hypnosis the client has reached. Recognizing levels will enable you to utilize what is happening, and to anticipate and head off possible reactions of distress.

Early in my practice, I was doing a Parts Integration (an NLP technique used to resolve Conscious/Unconscious conflicts) with a client who happened to be in a profoundly deep trance. As my client was having a very deep discussion with parts of her Unconscious, she found she was almost unable to move. I had missed the physiological signs of her shift into a deeper trance level. If I had noticed the level, I could have applied utilization and said, "You may notice that you are in a deep, deep trance, and do not want to move. This will probably amuse and delight you." Instead the client noticed on her own that she could not move, and this greatly distressed her.

Noticing signs of the level of trance will enable you to guide the client smoothly to a satisfying outcome. Not recognizing the level of trance could result in the client thinking in panic, "Oh no, I am totally relaxed and I can't move. What happens if I never become unrelaxed?" There is no need for them to feel this distress in trance.

Table: Stages of Hypnosis
(adapted from LeCron, *Hypnotism Today*, 1964)

The best indicator of the level of trance a client has reached is the hypnotic phenomena they have produced at your suggestion. The table on the next page is a useful guide to stages of hypnosis and the phenomena you can usually expect to induce at those stages. You will find a detailed discussion in the text that follows the table.

Stages of Hypnosis	
(Adapted from LeCron, 1964)	

Lethargy
 	
    Relaxation
 	
    Eye Catalepsy
 	
Catalepsy of Isolated Muscle Groups (Arm Catalepsy)
 	
    Heavy or Floating Feelings
 	
    Catalepsy of Complete Muscle Groups (Full Body Catalepsy)
	Light
	20%

Hypnotic Rapport
Medium
 	
    Smell and Taste Changes
 	
    Number Block
 	
Amnesia
 	
    Glove Anesthesia
 	
    Analgesia (No Pain)
	60%

Automatic Movement
 	
Positive Hallucinations – Visual and Auditory
 	
    Bizarre Post-Hypnotic Suggestions
 	
Anesthesia (No Feelings)
 	
    Negative Hallucinations
 	
    Comatose State
	Deep
	20%

There are three excellent ways to understand the continuum of trance levels:

1. seeing the six stages of hypnosis demonstrated,
2. experiencing the stages yourself,
3. taking a client through the stages.

When you begin to induce trance, the client will typically start at Stage 1 of hypnosis, experiencing **lethargy**, then some **relaxation**. The first catalepsy that you induce will usually be in the eyelids. This is because the muscles controlling the eyelids form one of the smallest muscle groups in the body and are easily relaxed. **Eyelid catalepsy** occurs when the client's eyes are so relaxed that they cannot open them; they will seem to be stuck shut. Eyelid catalepsy is an excellent convincer to prepare the client for deeper stages of hypnosis.

As the client moves into Stage 2 of hypnosis, you can elicit **catalepsy of isolated muscle groups**, such as arm catalepsy. Also typical are **heavy or floating feelings**. This is still considered light trance. At the deep end of Stage 2, you can induce **catalepsy of complete muscle groups**, such as those in the legs, or even **full body catalepsy**. Complete muscle group catalepsy is the beginning of medium trance.

In Stage 3, the client will exhibit a specific level of rapport, called **hypnotic rapport**, defined as *the state in which the client hears and sees only the Hypnotherapist*. In this stage, you can induce dramatic **smell and taste changes**. You can hold fresh cookies under the client's nose and tell them that it's old cabbage, and they will say, "Yuck." Or hold some ammonia under their nose and say it's fresh cookies, and they will say, "Mmmmm." You can also elicit **number block**, causing a number to disappear for a client. You can say, "The number *four* does not exist," and when you ask the client to count something, they will count, "One... two... three... five... six...." The number simply will not exist in their repertoire of numbers. (Be sure to put it back later.)

As the client moves to deeper levels of medium trance, they will be at Stage 4. At this level, you can produce **amnesia**, suggesting that the client forget portions of what happens in the trance.... This is very useful for post-hypnotic suggestions to help the client achieve desired changes without 'interference' from their Conscious Mind. You can also induce **glove anesthesia**, in which the hand becomes numb, as if you had put an anesthetic glove on it... or reduce sensations in some other part of the body. Just beyond glove anesthesia is **analgesia**, the absence of sensation of pain. When you have induced analgesia, the client can have ambiguous sensations, but no specific pain sensation. They will feel your touch, but not the pain of a needle jab.

At the deepest level of Stage 4 is **automatic movement**. The easiest automatic movement to initiate is with the client's hands. Simply start their hands rotating around each other in front of them, and they will automatically continue to rotate until you tell the client to stop. (Motor coordination can be imprecise during trance; you may need to guide the hands gently into the beginning of the movement.)

The client will begin to experience deep trance at the beginning of Stage 5. Common at this stage is **positive hallucination**, that is, seeing or hearing something that is not there. If you hold your empty hand in front of the client and tell them that you are holding a tennis ball, they will be able to tell you the color of the ball and the number that appears on it. (The opposite, negative hallucination, is *not* seeing or hearing something that *is* there. Negative hallucination comes into play in Stage 6).

A Stage 5 phenomenon familiar from stage hypnosis is **bizarre post-hypnotic suggestion**, which will cause the client to do something outlandish after they are out of trance, as long as it does not conflict with their values or beliefs. André Weizenhoffer tells a delightful story about post-hypnotic suggestion. Weizenhoffer said to a client in trance, "George, when you wake up, you will feel an irresistible urge to give me a dollar." George woke up and felt the urge; but he did not give Weizenhoffer the dollar. Weizenhoffer got a phone call the next morning at 2 a.m. from George, who said, "Darn it, André, I'm coming over to your house right now to give you two dollars." Weizenhoffer asked him, "Why didn't you give me a dollar at the time?" George said, "When I came out of the trance, I had this irresistible urge to give you a dollar. I knew that I would not have this urge normally, so I knew you must have given me a post-hypnotic suggestion. I said to myself, 'I'm *not* going to do it!' But I've been obsessing about it all night, so I'm coming over right now!"

When you give a post-hypnotic suggestion intended only for the time of the session, be sure to remove the suggestion before the client leaves!

At Stage 6 the client is reaching the deepest trance levels. At this stage, you can induce **anesthesia**, which would allow surgery without a chemical anesthetic or drilling of teeth without Novocaine. (If you induce anesthesia, I am *not* suggesting that you attempt the surgery or dentistry.) This is the level of trance that Dr James Esdaile induced by mesmerism to prepare patients for surgery in India in the 1800s. Taking the client to Stage 6 may require quite some time. They may need to go in and out of trance for an extended period in the process of deepening the hypnosis to this level.

At Stage 6, you can induce **negative hallucination**, or *not* seeing or hearing something that is there. If you are in perfect rapport, you can say to the client, "You only see me, you do not see or hear any-one else here." And if someone else were to stand in front of the client and talk, they would not have any awareness of that person.

Progressing deeper into Stage 6, the client will enter the **comatose** state. Dave Elman, whom we will be studying, calls this the Esdaile state. In this state, the client is sleeping deeply, yet still in hypnotic rapport with the Hypnotherapist.

At the deepest of level of Stage 6, **somnambulism**, or sleepwalk-ing, can occur. In the somnambulistic state the client can rise and move about, producing behaviour that looks almost as though they were awake. You would have to observe their behaviour closely to notice that they were not quite moving in the way an unhypnotized person would move.

In later chapters, we will discuss ways of inducing the hypnotic phenomena that are common to the six stages. To practise hypno-sis skilfully, you need to memorize the stages and the phenomena, so that recognizing them becomes second nature.

Applicability of the Stages of Hypnosis

The sequence of phenomena in the six stages is based on LeCron's and other hypnotists' research and experience with large numbers of clients. The LeCron scale is accepted as one of the major guides in hypnosis. This sequence will hold true for many, though not all, hypnotic subjects. Some clients will not experience all of the phenomena, and some may experience them in different order. For example, your client might achieve arm catalepsy not in light trance, but later, in medium or deep trance.

The percentages in the table show approximately what proportion of people can achieve each of the levels of trance in an early session without further conditioning. Of the people who come to see you, it is likely that 20% will initially achieve only light trance, 60% will achieve medium trance, and the remaining 20% will achieve deep trance.

Both Erickson and Dave Elman disputed these percentages. Erickson said he didn't know anybody who couldn't go into a deep trance, though some people took a long time to achieve it. His best subject actualized deep trance phenomena only after 300 repeated inductions. Erickson's point of view was that, "Trance is about learning how to go into trance."

LeCron's percentages referred specifically to people without previous practice at achieving trance. In my experience, anyone can eventually learn how to achieve deep trance, which assists a person in healing and making changes at the unconscious level.

You will improve your effectiveness as a Hypnotherapist by developing your own ability to experience trance at all three levels. You can practise by being a hypnotic subject or doing self-hypnosis. The Elman techniques (Chapter 16) are quite effective for reaching deep trance by self-hypnosis.

We are now ready to examine the most effective methods for leading a client into hypnosis. We will start with Milton Erickson's methods, in recognition of Erickson's pioneering work in the field, and because his methods are so often the most comfortable way to introduce a new client to trance.

Chapter 9

Ericksonian Methods

The Usefulness of Erickson's Techniques

Milton Erickson's greatest contribution to the field of hypnosis was his development of indirect, permissive techniques. He used hypnosis early in his practice of psychiatry, employing a classic direct, authoritarian approach from 1920 to 1940. Erickson had unusually sharp sensory acuity, which he developed even further with practice. Over the years, he combined his ability to sense the slightest physical signs with his intuitive counselling and story-telling skills, shifting gradually to a far more indirect approach. By the time of his death in 1980, he was doing almost all hypnosis indirectly. He sometimes did not even mention the word '*hypnosis*'; he might simply sit down and tell the patient some stories. The patient might leave wondering what had changed, only to find later that their problem had resolved itself.

Erickson believed that everyone is capable of achieving trance. He frequently said that trance is about learning how to go into trance. During the course of his life he had a great deal of practice—practising hypnosis daily from 1920 to 1980—and thus developed great expertise in inducing trance indirectly.

We don't have, or need, 60 years! Because Erickson left such clear teachings, we can study his techniques and model our methods on his.

Erickson's techniques are particularly effective for hypnotizing people who do not like to be told what to do, people who have hesitations about the process, and people who are being hypnotized for the first time. There are, of course, people who have spent most of their lives following orders. They may respond best to a direct, authoritarian approach. You will need to observe the client's responses before and during trance induction, and choose the approach that seems best suited. If you have any doubts about which approach to take, Erickson's techniques are an excellent way to start. If you find yourself using an approach that is not working, by all means switch to another type of induction.

You will sometimes encounter clients who are definitely *not* as suggestible as others. Erickson's methods may be the most effective way to reach them, following a suitable pre-talk. You can begin by telling them, "Trance is about learning how to go into trance... don't expect to feel hypnotized." Use the suggestibility tests as convincers. Then begin the induction, using indirect, permissive techniques. You will achieve a high rate of success.

Erickson's methods allow a client to feel wonderfully comfortable with the process of hypnosis. Erickson said that one of his best subjects became a good subject after 300 inductions. It is hard to imagine that he could have gotten the client to sit still for 300 inductions if he had not been using an approach that was comfortable and easy to relate to.

Not only is Erickson's approach comfortable for the client, it is also the easiest way for a new Hypnotherapist to begin inducing trance. When a new student learns a permissive approach to hypnosis before learning other techniques, they will install skills and beliefs that will increase their success rate with clients later in their career.

Erickson's Utilization Approach

Erickson's approach is a *utilization* approach, which has three stages.
- The first stage is *Preparation*, which we discussed in the chapters on personal history, pre-talk and suggestibility tests.
- The second stage is *Trance Work*, which will be our main focus in this chapter.
- The third stage is joint *Evaluation of Results* by the client and the Hypnotherapist, which locks in convincers for the client and enables deep integration of changes.

Steps in Trance Work

Essential to Trance Work is **fixation of the client's attention**. We have discussed how hypnotists from the time of James Braid had the client focus on an object positioned to make the eyes fixate in an upward stare. In contrast, Erickson achieved hypnosis by utilizing the client's beliefs and behaviour to focus their attention on inner realities. Using Milton Model patterns from Chapter 4, you too can engage the client's Unconscious Mind and focus their attention on inner realities.

The client comes to the Hypnotherapist with a fully developed 'model of the world,' which contains their values, their beliefs, and their concepts of how things work in the world. The client stores this model of the world in their Unconscious Mind. If the strongly held values and beliefs in their model conflict with their conscious desires, the client's unconscious model of the world will block their attainment of those desires. Hypnosis can unseat deeply held success-blocking beliefs that the client has about himself and his environment.

Erickson recognized that in order to help the client create changes, he first needed to **loosen the client's model of the world**, so that the client's Unconscious Mind would be open to changes in beliefs and values. While the client was in trance, Erickson used distraction, shock, surprise, doubt, confusion and any other process that challenged their model of the world. Erickson's purpose was to **lead the client into an unconscious search**. He used ambiguities, implications, questions, puns, and other indirect forms of suggestion to activate that unconscious search. The client would then move through an **unconscious process**, activating new associations and mental mechanisms. The client's **hypnotic responses**, often in the form of deep trance phenomena, would show Erickson that major change had occurred.

When you are obtaining your client's Personal History, your use of the Meta Model will begin loosening their model of the world by focusing their conscious attention on details that they have been deleting.

Here are specific questions to loosen the client's model and prepare them to move to new beliefs:

- What specifically do you want?
- Where are you now?
- What will you see, hear and feel when you have what you want?

- How will you know when you have it?
- What will this outcome get for you or allow you to do?
- Is it only for you?
- Where, when, how, and with whom do you want it?
- What resources do you need? What resources do you have now, and what do you need to get your outcome? Have you ever had this or done this before? Do you know anyone who has?
- Is the result that you want ecological? (That is, will it have positive, healthy effects on you and the people you relate to?) For what purpose do you want this? What will you gain or lose if you have it?

As you lead the client into trance, you can use Milton Model language to engage their Unconscious Mind in more profoundly loosening the model and becoming open to major change.

Ericksonian's Hypnotic Patterns of Indirect Suggestion

Erickson left us with a rich variety of hypnotic patterns to use in Trance Work. While you are developing your personal style, you can use this section as a reference to review these patterns.

1.   **Indirect suggestions**. The first major difference between Ericksonian hypnosis and other forms of hypnosis is that Ericksonian hypnosis is generally indirect rather than direct. A direct suggestion appeals to the Conscious Mind and invites evaluation. When you say, "Please close the window," the listener's conscious reaction is to choose between agreeing and disagreeing to do what you have asked.

An indirect suggestion resonates with the Unconscious Mind and is less likely to trigger evaluation. When you say,"I'm wondering if you can <u>close the window</u>," the listener's unconscious reaction is to hear your 'embedded' suggestion and follow it. Of course, a teenager might say,

"Yes," and walk away. Typically, however, "I'm wondering if you can close the window," will get the desired response.

2.   **Embedded commands**. Erickson often used embedded commands, or commands 'hidden' within longer sentences. If he said, "You don't need to <u>go into trance right now</u>," the client's conscious mind would be distracted by the surface sentence about not needing to go into trance, while their Unconscious Mind would hear and respond to the embedded command, "Go into trance right now."

Sometimes Erickson would combine an embedded command with punctuation ambiguity (as described earlier in the Milton Model) and say, "I want you to tell me only the things <u>you want to tell me everything</u>." The embedded command, "You want to tell me everything," would tend to bypass the Conscious Mind.

3.   **Embedded descriptions.** These are ways of thinking that work like embedded commands. If you are talking to a client about trance, you might say, "You may think that it's not <u>easy to go into a trance</u>. You may not find that <u>trance is delightfully relaxing</u>. Because you've never been in trance before, you don't know what to expect. In fact, you may not expect to <u>feel that calming, relaxing sensation that you are about to feel</u>." As the client is conscious of hearing things that they may not do, their Unconscious Mind will be hearing and responding to your embedded commands and descriptions.

There is no standard way to 'voice' embedded commands. In class, I often pause and change to a gravelly tone of voice to emphasize embedded commands, so that students can notice them easily. You may find it effective to pause and shift to a slightly deeper tonality, which might be very attractive to the client's Unconscious Mind. Try embedded commands with and without pauses just before them, with and without a change in tonality. Develop your own style of speaking embedded commands in any way that produces results.

4.   **Yes Sets**. Erickson used Yes Sets extensively to get the agreement of the client's Unconscious Mind. A Yes Set is a series of statements or questions that has the client saying or thinking, "Yes, yes, yes, yes, yes," so that when the Hypnotist adds a crucial instruction or question, the client again responds, "Yes."

> **Try this:**
> You are breathing. You are sitting here reading this book, and while you are doing that, you are probably thinking about certain things. Because you are interested in many things that have led you to study this subject, aren't you? That means that you will be able to learn hypnosis easily.

Notice how reading that paragraph felt in your body. I drew four automatic, effortless Yeses from your Unconscious Mind, so that my embedded command to learn hypnosis easily would glide smoothly into your Unconscious and get still another yes.

5.   **Truisms about sensations**. You can use a Yes Set of truisms about sensations to lead to a statement of what the client is feeling, and the client is likely to feel just what you have suggested. Here are some Ericksonian truisms: "Most people enjoy the refreshing coolness of a light breeze." "Many people find the sound of water very relaxing." "Some people blush easily when they recognize certain feelings about themselves." These truisms could be part of a Yes Set leading up to, "I wonder if you will feel absolutely comfortable and at peace recognizing your feelings about...."

As preparation for the next paragraph, I want you to notice something about your hands. Just for fun, put your hands on your lap. I want you to *really* feel your hands, and notice that one of your hands feels different from the other, doesn't it? Really notice this, one of your hands definitely feels different from the other.... It does. Do you know why one of your hands feels different from the other? *Because it is a different hand*. It is true. Look at your right hand, and look at your left hand.

Now if I say to the client, "In a moment, one of your hands is going to feel different from the other," the client is going to think in astonishment, "That's right... it *does*!" (I am not going to point out to the client that it is a different hand.) Once this convincer has entered the client's Unconscious Mind, I can add, "Most people can experience one hand as being lighter than the other," and my truism about sensation is a powerful suggestion paving the way to arm levitation and arm catalepsy.

6. **Truisms utilizing time**. Saying that something is about to happen (leaving the timing up to the client) is suggestive in itself and acts as a convincer when the thing happens. Everyone blinks fairly often. You can say to the client, "In a moment you're going to blink." When the client blinks, say, "That's right." The client's Unconscious Mind will think, "Interesting, they said I was going to blink, and I blinked. So I really did accept the suggestion." This makes the Unconscious Mind more amenable to future suggestions.

   Truisms utilizing time fit smoothly into double binds (described earlier in Chapter Four on the Milton Model), as in "Sooner or later, your eyes are going to close," or "Your headache can leave now... or as soon as your system is ready for it to leave."

7. **Not knowing, not doing**. Erickson often talked about not knowing or not doing: "You don't have to talk or move or make any sort of an effort. You don't even have to hold your eyes open. People can sleep and not know they are sleeping. They can dream and not remember the dream. You just do not know when the eyelids will close all by themselves. And you may not know just which hand will lift first." This paradoxical type of suggestion can be intriguing to the Unconscious Mind. You can suggest that it is fine for the client not to know or do something, and at the same time expand the Unconscious Mind's awareness of that something.

Whenever a client said, "I don't know," Erickson would say, "That's right, you don't know." He would validate the client's not knowing and not doing. In a sense, this is very Shamanistic.

8. **Open-ended suggestions**. Erickson used open-ended suggestions to invite the client's Unconscious Mind to supply all the details from the client's own experience. He might say: "We all have potential we are unaware of, and we usually don't know how it will be expressed." Or "You may not be aware of how much you are learning, and you are learning a lot. And it isn't right for me to tell you, 'Learn this,' or 'Learn that,' so you can learn whatever you want, in whatever order you wish."

9. **Covering all possible responses**. Erickson liked to describe a whole range of possibilities, so that no matter what happened, the client's attention would be focused on a sensation or movement in the range he described. He might say, "Soon you will find a finger or a thumb moving a bit, perhaps by itself. It can move up or down or to the side. It can be slow or quick, or it may not move at all." The client would eventually find a thumb or finger doing something, and this would act as a convincer. And no matter what the client did, they were right, for purposes of developing trance.

    This is one of my favorites: "Tonight when you sleep you may dream. You may have wild dreams… you may have exciting dreams… you may have mild dreams… you may have boring dreams. Your dreams may be memorable or they may not. In any case, let that be a sign… that you are integrating everything at the Unconscious level. So that by this time tomorrow, you will know everything you need to know in order to have the problem disappear."

10. **Questions to facilitate new response possibilities**. Erickson was also fond of using questions to focus attention or facilitate internal change. With a client who had been hypnotized before, he would ask, "Did you experience the hypnotic state as basically similar to the waking

state or different from the waking state?" In response, the client would *go back into trance* to compare the two possibilities. Similarly, we can induce trance just by asking, "Have you ever been in a trance before... *right now*?"

Ericksonian questions can facilitate internal change with a very suggestive double bind, giving the illusion of choice: "What will be the more effective way for you to lose weight? Will it be because you simply forget to eat? Or because you have little patience with heavy meals, since they prevent you from doing more interesting things?"

11.   **Compound suggestions**. Erickson used compound suggestions, in which one element was readily assumable or already happening, and the second element would gain in suggestive power by being connected with the first. There are several types of compound suggestions.

The simplest compound suggestion is the *Yes Set* with only one preparatory Yes: "It's such a beautiful day, let's go swimming."

Association creates almost instant trance simply by the fact that it is natural and nearly inevitable: "With every breath you take, you can become more aware of the natural rhythm in your body and feelings of comfort that develop."

Opposites form a compound suggestion, especially when one of the elements is already in progress: "As one hand lifts, the other can press down."

Tag questions and Why nots work well for regaining deep rapport with your client's Conscious and Unconscious Mind. They help dissolve any resistance which may be in the way of deeper levels of trance. In addition, they are perfect for Mismatchers. "And you are, aren't you?" "You can try, can't you?" "You can't stop it, can you?" "Why not let it happen?"

Negative + until suggestions release the client from feeling any pressure to 'perform.' "You don't have to go into a trance until you're ready. And you won't, until your Unconscious is ready." Released from worries about whether they are 'doing it right,' the client can go into a trance much more quickly.

Implications or If..., then... statements are also highly suggestive: "If you sit down, then you can go into a trance." "Now, if you uncross your legs and place your hands comfortably on your lap, you'll be ready to enter into a trance." Sometimes the ifs and thens are just implied: "As that comfort deepens, your Unconscious Mind can relax, while your Conscious reviews the nature of the problem; and when a relevant and interesting thought reaches your Conscious Mind, your eyes can open as you carefully consider it."

12.   **Double binds**. Erickson set up compelling double binds for his clients: "Would you like to enter into a trance now or later?" His attitude about double binds seemed to be, "I think my client should have the freedom to do exactly what I'm telling them, in any way that they like." The double bind appears to give a choice to the client.

The Conscious/Unconscious double bind is intriguingly truthful because, in fact, we have no way of knowing how much the Unconscious knows. You can say, "I think your Unconscious knows more about that than your Conscious Mind does. And if your Unconscious Mind knows more about that than your conscious Mind does, then you probably know more about it than you think you do."

A special instance of the double bind is double disassociation: "You can, as a person, awaken; but you do not need to awaken as a body. *(Pause)* You can awaken when your body awakens, but without recognition of your body. *(Pause)* Just awaken from the neck up."

These hypnotic patterns defined Erickson's indirect, permissive approach. In the next chapter, we will see many of them in the context of two examples of classic Ericksonian inductions.

Evaluation of Results

The third stage of the utilization approach is joint *Evaluation of Results* by the client and the Hypnotherapist. This might mean asking the client questions that will lead you and them to perceive the changes that have taken place. It might be a single direct question: *"That was a big one, wasn't it?"* The client's acknowledgment of changes will act as a powerful convincer, building confidence in the process and allowing deep integration of the changes they have made.

Here is one way to set up the client's evaluation of changes. When the client comes into the office with a certain unwanted behaviour, you can ask them to perform the behaviour in the office. For example,

Hypnotherapist:	"How do you know when it is time to smoke?"
Client:	"I have a feeling."
Hypnotherapist:	"Can you get that feeling of wanting to smoke now?"

If after your intervention the client cannot get in touch with the feeling of wanting to smoke, that result will act as a clear acknowledgment of the change.

By far the most powerful way for the client to acknowledge results is to *convince the Hypnotherapist* that they have changed.

Hypnotherapist:	"I don't think you have changed fully yet."
Client:	"No, I think I have."
Hypnotherapist:	"Really?"
Client:	"Yes!"
Hypnotherapist:	"Are you sure?"
Client:	"Yes, I am!"
Hypnotherapist:	"Good. Then you are sure you've changed."

Let the client convince you of the change whenever possible, and he will become more convinced of it himself.

Chapter 10

Two Ericksonian Inductions

We are ready to begin practical work in hypnosis. The best way to master hypnosis is to experience it as a client yourself and to practise simple inductions first, moving to more complex and elegant inductions later. Obviously, such practice requires a partner. Find one who shares your interest and enthusiasm so you can take turns. For learning purposes, detailed explanations follow some of the steps of the inductions below. (For later quick reference, these inductions are duplicated in the Appendix without explanations.)

Ericksonian Induction No. 1: Question Set Induction

We are going to begin with an induction called a *Question Set*, which will take about 10 minutes. By doing this induction and experiencing it as a subject, you will discover how to induce trance simply by asking questions. When you assume the Therapist's role, pay attention to what the client does each step of the way. Each time they exhibit trance-like behaviour, say, *"That's right,"* in a soothing and encouraging tone of voice.

1.	*Have you ever been in a trance before… right now?*
	To consider their answer, the client will have to 'try on' a trance. You have already explained trances like the driving trance or the elevator trance in the pre-talk. If the client answers "No," ask, "Can you remember the state you were in just before you completely woke up this morning?" or "Can you remember the last time you were completely absorbed in a book or a movie?"
2.	*Did you experience that state as being similar to the waking state, or different from the waking state?*
	You are asking the client to recall a trance state. Doing this is likely to lead them into trance.
3.	*Can you find a spot that you would like to look at comfortably?*

---

4. *As you continue comfortably looking at that spot for a while, do your eyelids want to blink?*

When they blink, say, *"That's right."* At this point or any other through Question 8, if the client's eyelids suddenly shut firmly and heavily, you can go right to Question 9.

5. *Will those lids begin to blink one at a time... twice or three times before they close altogether?*

As soon as you see a blink, pause in the questions and say, *"That's right."*

6. *Rapidly or more slowly?*

"That's right."

7. *Will they just close, now, or will they flutter all by themselves first?*

This is especially useful if the client's eyelids are fluttering, which is usually indicative of the first stage of hypnosis.

8. *Will the eyes close more and more as you get more and more relaxed?*

9. *That's right. Can those eyes just stay closed as you're comfortable to go deeper, just like when you go to sleep?*

10. *Or would you rather really try in vain and find you cannot?*

11. *And just when will you soon forget about them altogether because you're unconscious... wants you to dream!*

Insert suggestions.

Give your partner-client some suitable desired suggestions, such as, "You can integrate all the things you are
learning, and find it very easy to do hypnosis. Your
Unconscious Mind can supply to your Conscious Mind
whatever you need to know so you will be able to say
whatever you need to say in the moment, so that your
client will go deeply into trance."

Bring client out of trance: *In a moment, I am going to
count backwards from 10 to 1, and I want you to awaken
one tenth of the way with each number until you are fully
awake. 10... 9... 8... etc.*

Count back in whatever way you are most comfortable
with as the Hypnotherapist.

Physiological Responses to Trance

When you have done the induction for each other, consider what
you noticed while you were the client. You may have breathed
more deeply, or your breathing may have become more shallow.
We cannot set up specific physiological guidelines to gauge trance,
because people go into trance states differently. Even for the same
person, different trances can have different brain wave patterns,
different rates of respiration, different galvanic skin responses,
and different subjective experiences. Chapter 8 described hypnotic phenomena which typically correspond to various levels of
trance, but the correspondence between the phenomena and the
levels of trance can vary widely.

During trance the muscles relax in many different ways.
Sometimes the body moves into different positions. I have had
clients who looked as though they were about to fall off the chair,
but they did not. As the Hypnotherapist, you must pay attention
to your client's body posture and safety, especially if they are in
trance for a long period of time. You can give the client suggestions
for bodily safety: "You can relax your head... straighten your
neck... place your elbow gently on the armrest (especially for
eliciting ideomotor signals in trance)... relax your feet on the

floor... in an alignment that will bring you deepening comfort and support."

Sometimes trance is so comfortable that the client wants to stay in this peaceful state as long as possible. After you have suggested desirable changes for the client, you can give them suggestions to come out of trance.

With this first trance induction, you and your partner have begun to experience a powerful process for healing yourselves and others. The more easily you can go into trance, the more skilfully you will be able to use hypnosis in assisting your clients.

Ericksonian Induction No. 2: Arm Levitation

We are now going to expand on the first induction by *eliciting Arm Levitation* during the client's trance. You will again be inducing trance simply by asking questions. This time, however, you will want to pay close attention to the client's *breathing*. For the questions you ask to deepen the client's relaxation, *speak on the client's out-breath*. For the questions you ask to elicit arm levitation, *speak on the client's in-breath*. In this way, you will be using the client's own breathing to reinforce your suggestions physiologically.

To see how this breathing reinforcement works, put your feet flat on the floor and rest your hands and fingertips lightly on your thighs. Take a sharp, deep, full breath. Notice how your hands feel like they are lifting up.

As before, each time the client exhibits trance-like behaviour, say, *"That's right,"* in a soothing and encouraging tone of voice.

Out Breath

1.   *Have you ever been in a trance before...right now?*

       Asking Questions 1 and 2 on the client's out-breath will suggest relaxation while her breathing action supports it.

---

2.   *Did you experience that state as being similar to the waking state, or different from the waking state?*

In Breath

You can feel comfortable resting your hands gently on your thighs, can you not? (Demonstrate)

3.   *That's right, don't let them touch each other.*

When you ask this and the following questions on the client's in-breath, her breathing will give a light lift to the arms.

4.   *Can you let those hands rest so-oo lightly so that the fingertips just touch your thighs?*

Make sure the hands and fingertips barely touch the thighs.

5.   *That's right. As they rest there just so lightly, have you noticed yet how they tend to lift up a bit all by themselves* (Hypnotherapist, take a deep in-breath here) *with each breath you take? Good. Now we will just wait and see.*

Take several deep, full breaths. If you are in rapport with your client, the sound of your breathing will cause them to breathe with you. It may cause her arms to begin to lift. If this happens, move straight to Question 16. If the client's arms have not begun to lift, switch to speaking on her out-breaths and continue with Question 6.

Out Breath

6.   *Now, can you find a spot that you would like to look at comfortably?*

7.   *As you continue comfortably looking at that spot for a while, do your eyelids want to blink?*

8.   *Will those lids begin to blink one at a time... twice or three times before they close altogether?*

9.   *Rapidly or more slowly?*

10.   *Will they just close, now, or will they flutter all by themselves first?*

11.   *Will the eyes close more and more as you get more and more relaxed?*

12.   *That's right. Can those eyes just stay closed as you're comfortable to go deeper, just like when you go to sleep?*

13.   *Can your comfort go more and more deeply, inside, so that you'd rather not even try to open your eyes?*

14.   *Or would you rather really try in vain and find you cannot?*

15.   *And just when will you soon forget about them altogether because your unconscious... wants you to dream!... of lifting, lifting, lifting.*

In Breath

16.   *Have you noticed your hands lifting, lifting, lifting even more lightly, even more easily, and by them-selves... as the rest of your body relaxes more and more?*

     With Question 16, begin again speaking on the client's in-breaths. See the example that follows these questions to get the breathing exactly right.

17.   *As that goes on, does one hand or the other... or maybe both... continue lifting, lifting, lifting even more?*

18.   *And does that hand stay up and continue lifting, lifting, lifting even higher and higher all by itself? Does the other hand want to catch up with it and go up too, or will the other hand just relax in your lap?*

19.   *That's right. And does the hand continue lifting, lifting, lifting as it is, or will the lifting get smoother or less smooth as the hand continues upward toward your face?*

Vary what you say according to the client's movements!

20.   *Now... Does the hand slow down or go faster and faster as it approaches your face deepening your comfort? Will it... pause a bit before it finally touches your face so you'll know you are really going into a trance? And it won't touch until your Unconscious... is really, really ready to let you go deeper... will it?*

21.   *And... will your body automatically take a deeper breath when that hand touches your face and you really relax and experience yourself going deeper and deeper?*

Out Breath

22.   *That's right. And will you even bother to notice you're deepening the comfortable feeling as that hand slowly goes back to your lap all by itself? And will your Unconscious be in a dream by the time that hand comes to rest?*

Insert suggestions.

In Breath

Bring client out of trance: *"In a moment, I am going to count backwards from 10 to 1, and I want you to awaken one tenth of the way with each number until you are fully awake. 10... 9... 8... etc."*

The paragraph following this recaps Questions 16-21 to show how your breathing, head position and voice direction can reinforce your suggestions. With a little practice, this coordination of your breathing, speaking and movement will become natural and easy. You need to tilt your head forward, speaking to the client's stomach or feet. Just before each time you say the word *'lift,'* raise your head towards the ceiling while taking a deep, full, *audible* breath, so that *'lift'* is the first word you speak on your out-breath. The changing direction of your voice and the sound of your breathing will give powerful suggestions to the client's Unconscious Mind, causing them to match your breathing and your body movements. This will give lift to their arms!

(Start with head down.) *Have you noticed your hands* (move head up and breathe in) *lifting, lifting, lifting even more lightly, even more easily, and by themselves... as the rest of your body* (move head down and breathe out) *relaxes more and more? As that goes on, does one hand or the other... or maybe both... continue* (move head up and breathe in) *lifting, lifting, lifting even more?* (move head down and breathe out) *And does that hand stay up and continue* (move head up and breathe in) *lifting, lifting, lifting even higher and higher all by itself? Does the other hand want to catch up with it and go up too, or will the other hand* (move head down and breathe out) *just relax in your lap? That's right. And does the hand continue* (move head up and breathe in) *lifting, lifting, lifting as it is, or will the lifting get smoother or less smooth as the hand continues upward toward your face? Now.... Does the*

---

hand slow down or go faster and faster as it approaches your face deepening your comfort? Will it... pause a bit before it finally touches your face so you'll know you are <u>really</u> going into a trance? And it won't touch until your Unconscious... is really, really ready to let you go deeper... will it? And... will your body automatically take a deeper breath (keep head up and breathe in) *when that hand touches your face and you really relax and experience yourself going deeper and deeper?*

You will often want to ad-lib this series of questions. Some clients' hands may rise a couple of inches, and some may go all the way to their faces. Any time the hand comes off the leg, you have a successful arm levitation.

Chapter 11

Ericksonian Interventions

The purpose of our first two Ericksonian inductions was to provide practice for you, the Hypnotherapist, in inducing trance and in teaching your client how to go into trance. In this chapter, we will discuss steps for an Ericksonian intervention to assist the client in making changes they want to make. These steps will form a general hypnosis paradigm that can serve as a model for much of the hypnotherapy you offer.

I use a combination of Time-Line Therapy®, NLP techniques and hypnosis in working with clients. These three systems overlap and complement each other. I generally use hypnosis when I am guiding a client in physical healing or when I cannot complete an intervention using Time-Line Therapy® or NLP techniques.

Whereas Neuro-Linguistic Programming offers a variety of *specific* interventions, hypnosis is a *generalized* intervention. For example, in NLP we may anchor a resourceful state, change an unsuccessful strategy, shift a client's values, or integrate conflicting parts of the client's Unconscious. Each of these interventions targets a specific area of the Unconscious the way a surgical procedure targets a specific area of the body.

A hypnotic intervention has a broader transformative scope. In hypnosis, we usually give more generalized suggestions for accomplishing the desired change. Consider the example of a client who has the problem of excessive impulse buying. Using NLP, we might intervene by changing the specific buying strategy the client uses. Using hypnosis, however, we might give a strong general suggestion that the client will no longer buy unneeded items.

There are hundreds of books available on how to do hypnotherapy. The American Institute of Hypnotherapy offers 111 courses on hypnosis, and each of these courses is based on a different book. Well over half the books currently in print include specific ways of doing interventions. Many of them provide scripts. If you have access to the Internet, you will find over 100 scripts at our web site:

http://www.hypnosis.com

Though you may often want to use a script for a specific situation, the general hypnosis paradigm we are about to discuss will prepare you to work confidently without a script in many cases.

Milton Erickson would generally interview a new client a week before doing the first intervention with them. During the ensuing week, he would customize an intervention for the client, working from his case notes and outlines of possible things to say. In designing interventions for your clients, you will find the following paradigm useful.

General Hypnosis Paradigm

A. **Preparation**. Define desired outcome. Obtain personal history. Accomplish pre-talk and suggestibility tests. (See Chapters 6, 7.)

B. **Induction**. Use a formal or informal trance induction. (See Chapters 10, 14, 16, 17.)

C. **Utilization**. Utilize all of the client's behaviour to help them achieve and deepen trance. Observe hypnotic phenomena to gauge client's level of trance. (See Chapters 5, 8.)

Change Work

See notes beginning on next page for detailed explanations of the following 6 steps.

As you follow these steps, change the wording to fit the situation, rather than referring generally to 'the problem.'

1.	Does your Unconscious Mind know what to do to solve the problem?
2.	Is it possible for your Unconscious Mind to heal the condition?

3.   Is it all right to heal this now or to organize the steps now for healing?

4.   Are there any other problems your Unconscious Mind would like to work on?

5.   Unconscious Mind, go ahead and heal (client's name).

6.   How quickly will your Unconscious Mind start the healing? How quickly will it finish?

Bringing the Client Out

In a moment, I am going to count backwards from 10 to 1, and I want you to awaken one tenth of the way with each number until you are fully awake. 10... 9... 8... etc.

Notes on Steps for Change Work

Step 1. *Does your Unconscious Mind know what to do to solve the problem?* Does it know how to assist the client in having the problem disappear? About three-quarters of the time, the Unconscious Mind will answer "Yes." This answer is a sign to both you and the client that the client is establishing rapport with their Unconscious.

If the Unconscious Mind says it does *not* know how to solve the problem, you need to get the client in touch with additional resources. One of the main tenets of Ericksonian hypnosis is, "Our clients have all the resources they need to solve whatever problems they bring to us." In this case, the added resource may be the Higher Self. You can ask,

> *"Can your Unconscious Mind get in touch with the blueprint of perfect health and healing that exists in the Higher Self and transfer it to the blueprint that the Unconscious Mind uses to create the body?"*

Whether or not you believe that there is a Higher Self (and whether or not the client believes it), the client's Unconscious Mind will usually respond positively to this question and find that it then knows how to solve the problem!

If the Unconscious Mind does not respond to this appeal to the Higher Self, I usually move to Time-Line Therapy®, which can readily be introduced while the client is in trance. If you need information on Time-Line Therapy®, you will find a full description of methods in my book *Time-Line Therapy and the Basis of Personality*.

Step 2. *Is it possible for your Unconscious Mind to heal the condition?* As before, if the answer is "No," ask the Unconscious Mind to get in touch with the blueprint of perfect health and healing that exists in the Higher Self. Assume that it is possible for the Unconscious Mind to heal virtually anything that the client has brought to you as a presenting problem. My personal experience—and countless experiments in hypnosis documented since the 1860s—show that once we enlist the aid of the Unconscious Mind, miraculous things can be done.

If you have unlimited beliefs about what your client can do and you describe your beliefs in terms that the client can relate to, you can play a powerful role in facilitating the client's changes. Of course, the ultimate responsibility for changes rests with the client. The changes they accomplish will result from their own communication with their Unconscious Mind. I regularly tell my clients, "You *can* do anything, but whether or not you actually *do*, depends on your ability to communicate with your Unconscious Mind. I'm here to help you develop that ability."

Step 3. *Is it all right to heal this now or to organize the steps now for healing?* Sometimes the Unconscious Mind will know what to do and will acknowledge that the desired change is possible, but will feel that it is not alright to go ahead and make the change.

If we accept the paradigm that the Unconscious Mind has the well-being of the body as a prime concern, this seems contradictory. There are several reasons that the Unconscious might not consider it all right to solve the problem. The Unconscious Mind can get into a mode where it is mistaken about what it is supposed to do, as the result of a stream of misleading messages filtering in through the Conscious Mind: "Do this. Feel this."

In processing continuous input from the media, the Conscious Mind can get fixated on disease. Every day, TV news programmes feature stories about diseases, giving the Conscious Mind far more information about disease than about health. Advertising for Cold Capsules announces that "Cold and flu season is here." People comply by catching the flu. The media's focus on disease can convince an Unconscious Mind that it is not its job to be well. But typically, when reminded that its highest job is to preserve the body, the Unconscious Mind will come around to acknowledging and doing that job. My recommendation is that you work with the Unconscious Mind and remind it of its magnificent purpose.

In other situations, the client's Unconscious Mind may think that they are guilty of something and need to be punished. You will need to lead the client in working through the guilt, using Time-Line Therapy® or reframing the incident to which the client attaches guilt.

In getting the client's Unconscious Mind to acknowledge that it is all right to solve a problem, skill in *reframing* is very useful. Reframing consists of leading the client to see a different context or a different meaning for a behaviour—either their own or someone else's. This is a key skill in hypnotherapy and NLP.

My NLP Practitioner and Master Practitioner training includes step-by-step information on how to do reframing. I recommend Erickson and Rossi's book *Life Reframing in Hypnosis*. Leslie LeCron's book *Self Hypnotism* will also give you valuable information about reframing and the working of the Unconscious Mind.

Step 4. *Are there any other problems your Unconscious Mind would like to work on?* The Unconscious Mind may have its own agenda of things it needs to work on. If it responds "Yes" to this question, you need to find out what else it wants to work on and loop back up to Step 1.

Step 4 is an optional question. I skip this question if I am working on a life-threatening disease with a client. On the other hand, if the client has come to me for help in losing weight, I would certainly ask their Unconscious Mind, "Are there any other problems you would like to work on?"

Step 5. *Unconscious Mind, go ahead and heal (client's name).* Sometimes the Unconscious Mind knows what to do and acknowledges that it is possible and all right for it to do it, but feels it does not have permission from the Conscious Mind.

Most people give their Unconscious Minds conflicting information on a regular basis. Examples might be that one day a certain person is wonderful and the next day they are no good; one day you like someone and the next day you don't. The Unconscious Mind gets confused about this because it takes literally everything that you tell it and think about. You give the Unconscious Mind clear permission in Step 5, so that it knows to go ahead and heal the condition.

Step 6. *How quickly will the Unconscious Mind start the healing? How quickly will it finish?* Typically, you need to give the Unconscious Mind some parameters right away. If you are working on a physiological condition, such as a bleeding ulcer, you need to say to the Unconscious, "How quickly will you start to heal this condition? Sometimes Unconscious Minds like to begin healing things like ulcers right away; and sometimes they like to take a long, long time to start the process, maybe as long as 24 hours. Which would you prefer?" The Unconscious Mind will then give you a start time.

Then say to the Unconscious Mind, "How long will it take you to finish the healing process? Sometimes Unconscious Minds like to finish the healing process in a relatively short time, like as little as...." Now your knowledge of the body comes into play. If you are going to do physiological work, you ought to read Deepak Chopra's *Quantum Healing*. It has a number of metaphors about how quickly the Mind/Body unit can heal itself. In the case of a bleeding ulcer, we have a brand new stomach lining every five days. Therefore, a bleeding ulcer can totally disappear in five days.

If the Unconscious Mind does not want to start healing right away, do you encourage it to, or do you give it as much time as it needs? I prefer giving the Unconscious Mind reasonable parameters and then let it choose the time it wants to take to start. The way I see it, sometimes an Unconscious Mind may have a list of things on its agenda already and may need to finish those. So it may say, "Well, my dance card is full today, but I can certainly start tomorrow at noon."

Case History

A client came to see me with a bleeding ulcer. As I worked through the 6 steps described above, the client's Unconscious Mind told me, "Yes, I know what to do to heal the ulcer. It is possible. It is OK." I said, "OK, Unconscious Mind, how quickly will you start to heal this ulcer? Sometimes Unconscious Minds like to begin healing things like ulcers right away, and sometimes they like to take a long, long time to start the process, maybe as long as 24 hours. How long will you take?"

The client's Unconscious Mind replied, "I'd like to start right away." I said, "How quickly will you finish? Sometimes Unconscious Minds like to finish the healing process in as short as five days. Sometimes Unconscious Minds like to take a long, long time to finish healing, like seven days."

The Unconscious Mind said it would take 7 days to heal the bleeding ulcer. When the client went to the doctor 7 days later, there was no trace of the ulcer. That is not anything miraculous. We simply enlisted the aid of the client's Unconscious Mind to do the healing.

What was interesting was that my client wrote me three months later and sounded totally empowered by the process. He said, "I had recreated my bleeding ulcer. This time I decided I was as good as you were, Tad. I figured I could get rid of it myself, and so I did!" The exciting thing

---

was that the client could now talk directly to his Unconscious Mind without my help. He was fully able to heal himself, drawing on a closer, deeper relationship with his Unconscious Mind.

Chapter 12

The Pendulum and
Other Ideomotor Signals

The General Hypnosis Paradigm in Chapter 11 is a pattern for carrying on a dialogue with the client's Unconscious Mind while the client is in trance. A pendulum can be a useful tool for facilitating the dialogue when the client has not yet displayed some of the deeper trance phenomena, or when they want relief from a problem and are not yet ready to deal with the underlying cause.

Case History

Here is an example of how I have used a pendulum with great success. A woman came to me who had been brutally attacked by a mugger three days earlier. Each night since the mugging, she had awakened screaming. Although it was agony for her to talk about the incident, she was very willing to go into a trance to get rid of the problem. Her desired outcome was to sleep through the night, feeling rested upon awakening.

I hung a pendulum from the woman's finger, and began a discussion with her Unconscious Mind via the pendulum. I asked, "Can I please have a signal for 'Yes.' And can I please have a signal for 'No?'" The pendulum clearly swung in opposite directions to show her Unconscious Mind's responses.

I asked, "Does your Unconscious Mind know what to do to sleep soundly through the night?" Her Unconscious signalled, "Yes."

I asked, "Is it possible to release any negative emotions necessary to get rid of this problem, so you can sleep through the night?" Her Unconscious Mind responded, "Yes."

I continued, "Is it OK to release those negative emotions?" The Unconscious Mind gave me a clear, "Yes."

I said, "OK, Unconscious Mind, go ahead. How quickly would you like to start the process of releasing the negative emotions? Sometime Unconscious Minds like to start right away and sometimes they like to take as much as 12 to 24 hours to begin the process. Would you like to start right away?"

The Unconscious Mind signalled, "No." I liked the "No" at that point, because it showed me that the woman's Unconscious Mind was really considering what to do.

"Would you like to start in 12 hours?" Her Unconscious replied, "Yes."

I continued, "Sometimes Unconscious Minds like to finish processes like this very, very quickly, like in as little as 24 hours. Sometimes they like to take a long, long time to solve problems like this, for example as much as 48 hours. Would you like to finish in 48 hours?" A clear "No."

"Would you like to finish in 24 hours?" Again, "No."

I tried once more: "Would you like to finish in less than 24 hours?" Still, "No." I was at least pleased that we were communicating.

I asked, "Would you like to finish in 36 hours?" And the woman's Unconscious Mind, via the pendulum, showed an unhesitating "Yes."

That night the woman woke up and screamed. The following night and every night after, she slept through the night and awakened rested. This was a very general intervention with the Unconscious Mind, in that I asked her Unconscious Mind to simply let go of whatever it needed to let go of, so that the client could be comfortable. From the point of view of Time-Line Therapy®, this intervention did not handle the root cause…. In fact, the client was not ready to handle it. What I recommended was that the client get help in handling the traumatic material once she was comfortable enough to do that.

When to Use a Pendulum

When a client asks for help with a presenting problem, very often neither you nor the client will be aware of the mental source of the problem. In doing an intervention, Erickson regularly focused not only on clearing up the presenting problem, but on handling the underlying concerns of the patient's Unconscious Mind. Otherwise, the problem might readily recur.

If you use a pendulum intervention, for example, to help a client heal a bleeding ulcer, unless you have dealt with the root cause of the ulcer, the client may re-manifest it later. The most effective intervention I know for leading a client to heal a physical condition is to first use Time-Line Therapy® to deal with the mental source of the condition, and then use hypnosis, possibly with a pendulum, to address the physical condition itself.

I carry a pendulum with me all the time, because it is a useful tool for working with a client who has difficulty going into trance, or cannot do Time-Line Therapy® due to lack of concentration, inability to visualize, or resistance to floating above their Time-Line. The pendulum of itself can facilitate a trance induction. Also, as the client begins to see the responses their Unconscious Mind is making, the pendulum is a powerful convincer.

How to Use a Pendulum

You need two items for a pendulum intervention: the pendulum itself, and a pendulum chart.

It is best to have a pendulum that hangs from a finger clip. (See picture on page 108.) This will keep the pendulum steadily fixed on the finger and allow it to swing freely. It will also avoid the client's being distracted by the need to hold on to a string or chain. You can find this type of pendulum at a New Age bookstore or order one from Advanced Neuro Dynamics at 1-800-800-6463.

You may copy the following pendulum chart.

Pendulum Chart

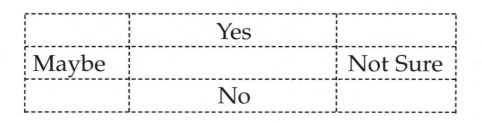

	Yes	
Maybe		Not Sure
	No	

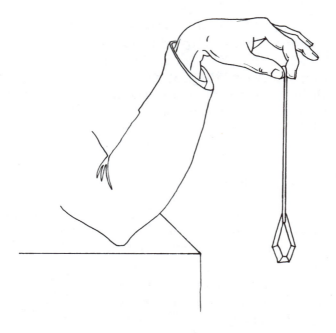

Begin by showing the client how to sit and hold their arm to use the pendulum, with their elbow resting on a stable surface (a table-top or desk is best). The forearm should be almost vertical, suspended in mid-air. The hand should be totally relaxed, hanging from the wrist. (See picture on page 108.)

In moving the client's arm and hand to this position, you can induce arm catalepsy (or 'waxy flexibility') by applying in your *touch* the principle that "ambiguity in any representational system will cause trance to occur." Touch the client's hand very lightly in guiding their forearm to the vertical position. In fact, touch the hand so lightly that your touch is *ambiguous,* meaning that the client is not sure of the very last moment in which your touch occurred. While their Unconscious Mind is fixed on this ambiguous touch, leave the arm suspended in mid-air.

This arm catalepsy induction, from Erickson and Rossi's *Experiencing Hypnosis*, will increase your client's comfort in using the pendulum and make the process more likely to be successful.

With the client's arm cataleptic, clip the pendulum on their pointer finger. If this is the first time the client is using a pendulum, you will be getting their Unconscious Mind used to some new sensations as you instruct it how to respond. You need to ask the client's Unconscious Mind to choose three signals: "Yes," "No," and "Not consciously ready to know yet."

Begin by saying to the client, "Can your Unconscious Mind give me a signal for 'Yes' that is easy to see? Sometimes Unconscious Minds like to give me a signal for 'Yes' like this." Take the pendulum and hold it out almost horizontal, and then let it swing back and forth in a wide arc. Say, "This would be a perfectly appropriate signal."

Continue by saying, "And sometimes Unconscious Minds like to give me a signal for 'Yes' that is easy to see, like this." This time let the pendulum swing in the opposite direction, saying, "This would also be a perfectly appropriate signal."

This demonstration gives the Unconscious Mind and the finger the feeling or the *kinesthetics* of the swing.

Now say to the client, "Please ask your Unconscious Mind to show us a signal for 'Yes.' Then repeat inside your head several times, 'Signal for Yes, Signal for Yes.' That's right." Allow plenty of time. If after waiting you see only an ambiguous or very weak signal, say, "Good. Now can your Unconscious Mind go ahead and amplify that signal so it is very easy to see. That's right."

If you are using the pendulum chart, place it under the pendulum now, aligning it to correspond to the 'Yes' signal.

Now repeat the process to elicit signals for "No" and "Not Consciously Ready To Know Yet." Very often, though not always, "Yes" and "No" will be exact opposite directions corresponding to the crossed lines on the chart. Sometimes the Unconscious Mind will give circular signals, swinging the pendulum clockwise or counterclockwise... or both. Acknowledge and encourage the Unconscious Mind: "Thank you very much, Unconscious Mind, for communicating so helpfully."

Once you have set up a system of clear signals with the client's Unconscious Mind, follow the General Hypnosis Paradigm from Chapter 11.

Additional Notes on use of the Pendulum

With some clients it works better to induce trance first and then introduce the pendulum. Most clients, however, use the pendulum well without any formal trance induction. This provides a great advantage with clients who initially resist entering trance.

The pendulum is a biofeedback device. It works through the integration of Conscious and Unconscious processes. This means the client needs to see the pendulum and its signals. Their consciousness of the movements of the pendulum sets the stage for their Unconscious Mind to communicate through this medium.

Sometimes the client will be concerned about interfering with the signals from their Unconscious Mind. They may say, "I'm not sure I trust the answers I am getting," or "I just don't trust my Conscious Mind not to interfere." If this is the case, you can tell the client, "Simply do not interfere with the pendulum. Hold a neutral thought in your mind and let whatever happens, happen."

If the client is still concerned, as you are asking a question, block their view with a piece of paper. This means actually holding a piece of paper between the client's face and the pendulum. The moment the client begins to answer, pull the piece of paper away, so they can see the swing of the pendulum. This will maintain the biofeedback nature of the process.

The pendulum has proved to be an excellent avenue to having a full conversation with the Unconscious Mind without deep trance.

Other Ideomotor Signals

The pendulum is most often used with the assistance of another person. There are two other ideomotor signals (that is, body movements that carry a message from the Unconscious Mind) that can easily be practised alone, without being noticeably in trance. I generally teach these to kids for use in school, but anyone can use them.

The first signal is called '**Sticky.**' This is mainly for "Yes-No" questions. Take a plastic notebook. Touch the top padded part of your pointer-finger to the waxy plastic covering of the notebook.

Rub your finger back and forth sideways along the edge, fairly quickly. Ask your Unconscious Mind for a "Yes" signal. Rub back and forth again, asking for a "No" signal. Notice the difference in the drag of your finger across the plastic for the two answers. Once you have established "Yes" and "No," concentrate on one question at a time, and use Sticky to let your Unconscious Mind tell you the answer. Each of the students to whom I have taught Sticky has seen at least a full point increase in their grade average!

The second signal is called '**ABCD.**' This is mainly for answering multiple-choice test questions. For ABCD use your non-dominant hand. Rest the heel of that hand on your knee, so that your fingers are hanging loose. The fingers should not touch the knee because you want to get the full ideomotor response. With attention focused on your fingers, ask your Unconscious Mind, "Give me a signal for A." Wait for the signal... a slight movement of one finger. "Give me a signal for B." Wait for the signal. After seeing the signals for all four answers, concentrate on a multiple-choice question and watch your fingers for the response. Can you imagine how valuable ABCD is in a classroom setting? One of our students who taught this signal to his nephew reports that the nephew scored a "96" on a multiple-choice science examination for which the highest grade up to that point had been an "85."

Is this cheating? How do we know the student has learned anything? My response is that all learning, behaviour, and change takes place in the Unconscious Mind. All we are doing is finding effective ways to communicate with the Unconscious Mind and access the information which is already stored in it. There is no cheating involved here! The fact is that the Unconscious Mind faithfully records everything that we experience. If you can simply tune in to the Unconscious Mind, you have access to any answer you need.

With clients I prefer to use the pendulum rather than Sticky or ABCD, because the movement of the pendulum is so easy to observe. During a school test, however, you cannot have your son or daughter say, "Excuse me, I'm going to get out my pendulum!"

Chapter 13

Metaphors

In Chapter 4, we discussed the hypnotic language patterns of the Milton Model, which Erickson developed for use in a permissive, indirect style for inducing trance. We noted that the key principle underlying Milton Model patterns is that *ambiguity in any representational system causes trance.*

Over the years, Erickson discovered that he could lead a patient into trance without any formal induction by telling stories that would engage the curiosity of the patient's Unconscious Mind, opening a channel for direct dialogue with the Unconscious. These stories are *metaphors.*

In this chapter, you will be reading examples of metaphors. They will include *words in italics* in many places. The *italics* are not for emphasis, but for drawing your attention to words or phrases that are examples of Milton Model patterns from Chapter 4 or Ericksonian techniques, such as embedded commands, from Chapter 9. The margins in this chapter will give references to loops. We will discuss loops later in the chapter.

Multiple Embedded Metaphors

Open Loop No.1

Now it took Erickson a long time to *develop the smoothest ways to put a patient in touch with their Unconscious Mind.* Think about this for just a minute. He was in practice doing hypnosis every single day, from 1920 until his death in 1980. And during that period of 60 years, he would often see 14 patients a day, sometimes 7 days a week. Now the way I see it, if you did that, you'd *get pretty good at hypnosis* too. You'd *figure out what to do* after a while, and what Erickson said was, "It took me a long time to learn this, but once I learned it, my hypnosis became a lot better. I was much more easily able to *facilitate trance* in my patients. And I realized that most of what needs to happen in hypnosis is utilization. We need to discover and utilize already occurring phenomena that the patient brings to the hypnotic session." And so he said, "Whereas during the early days, I would tell the client what to do, saying, '*Go into a trance,*' now I don't say that any more." He said, "One of the things I did in the process of learning how to *communicate with the Unconscious Mind* was that in the early days, I actually sat down at a typewriter and typed out 30 pages of notes." Imagine that. "Single spaced, narrow margins, typewritten pages, with all the things I could say to show a patient how to *go into a trance easily.* And," he said, "with experience as I continued my practice, I was able to reduce that to *25 pages, and then 20, and then 15, and then 10, and then 9 pages, 8 pages, and then 7, then 6, then 5, and 4, and 3, and then 2, and then 1.* And then," he said, "I could reduce it to one paragraph, and then one sentence, and then I realized I didn't need to use words at all. What I discovered was that by utilizing the naturally occurring states in a client, I could begin to assist the client to *go deeply into trance."*

And so what is really important as we discuss Ericksonian hypnosis is the ability to look at a person and see what state they are in... and *anticipate things they are about to do* before they are aware of those things themselves. This is Utilization, as we discussed in Chapter 5. Utilization depends on your ability to *pay attention to details.*

Open Loop No.2

And if I could give you a gift, it would be the gift of curiosity. I don't know if you *remember when you were a kid,* but when I was a kid, my dad used to hide the Christmas presents in the closet in his bedroom. And I always wanted to know what they were. *Didn't you?* So, I'd wait.... I grew up in Syracuse where there's lots of snow, and when my parents would go outside to shovel the driveway, I'd run over to the bedroom, over to my Dad's closet, and I'd pull up a chair. Then I'd look out the window and see how they were doing. Then I'd run back and reach way up and grab the biggest present. And what's the first thing you do with a present? Shake it.... *'Cause you want to know what's inside.* Then you look at the outer wrapper. And you can tell a lot of things from outer wrappers, *can't you?* You can. And you see what else you can notice. Like, is the box heavy, is the paper thin? Which store did it come from? After a while you begin to *notice that certain wrappers are thin enough to see through.* And, if you really *feel daring,* and if you feel you have a lot of time, from time to time, you might just peel the paper back a little way, carefully, hoping not to rip the wrapping. You did this, I know you did...hoping not to rip the wrapping paper and then you look inside. If I could give you a gift, it would be that kind of curiosity, that kind of curiosity about what in the world is going on over there, as you *look at your client*, as you *pay close attention to every detail*.

Open Loop No.3

In fact, Erickson tells a wonderful story that is written up in the book *My Voice Will Go With You*, by Sidney Rosen. One of Erickson's students, whom we will call John, was fascinated by hypnosis and wanted to *learn everything there is to know about it*. Erickson told John to *pay close attention*, very close attention to the people around him. John was in college, and one day a professor said to him, "John, how are you going to do on the test?" And John said, "I'll do very well, Professor, because you only have 10 questions, and they are... " And John proceeded to name the 10 questions. Now the professor was shocked, and said, "John, you've obviously gone into my desk, because not only do you know the 10 questions, but you know them in order. We are going to the Dean." So he took John to the Dean and the Dean said, "John, have you been cheating?" And John said, "No, I haven't and I can prove it. Please send someone to my room to get my notebook." So they sent another student to John's room to get his notebook. When the student brought it back, they opened it up and found that John had taken incredibly good notes. *Next to some things he'd put one asterisk, and next to some things he'd put 2 asterisks, and next to some things he'd put 3, and next to some, 4... or 5, and next to some, 6... but only next to a few things did John put 7 asterisks, and they weren't numbered 1, 2, 3, 4, 5.* No, no. The first one was 6, the second was 1, and the third was 4, and so on. And John said, "You know, you can tell a lot by paying attention to what a professor is saying, because they all have their own ideas about what they like and what they don't like." And he said, "All I did was *pay attention, and listen carefully to his tone of voice, and look at him*." You know, Erickson thought that John was one of his best students. Now in fact, he was always telling students to *pay attention* to things they normally did not pay attention to... things that other people said and did. He knew that by paying attention, they could begin to turn on the power of their client's Unconscious Mind.

Open Loop No.4

One of the most dramatic examples of the power of the Unconscious is given in the book *The Psychobiology of Mind/Body Healing*, where Ernest Rossi writes about a case that was reported in the *Journal of The American Medical Association*. Mr. Right was a lung cancer patient in the '50s, when the drug Krebiozen was introduced. He had had cancer for quite some time, and was convinced that somewhere along the way, there would be a drug that would cure him and he would finally *be healed*. He was on oxygen and had less than three months to live, in the opinion of his doctors. Krebiozen was announced and Mr. Right's hospital was given the authorization to use Krebiozen in the first round of testing. The doctor decided to use Mr. Right as one of his test patients, even though he didn't quite meet the criteria of being able to participate in the test. Mr. Right was given Krebiozen on a Friday for the first time. His doctor left for the weekend, leaving instructions with the nurses to administer Krebiozen till Monday.

When he came back on Monday, the doctor was amazed to find Mr. Right out of his bed and walking around the cancer ward telling all the other patients the wonders of Krebiozen. Understandably excited, the doctor examined Mr. Right immediately and found remarkable improvements. Then he hurried to examine the other patients in the ward who had also received Krebiozen. With the other patients, he found no change.

Mr. Right's injections continued. After a month or two, he was well enough to leave the hospital. He returned to his hobby of flying his private plane, which was not equipped with a pressurization system. Because of the fact that Mr. Right was flying at 12,000 feet, his doctor judged that his lung cancer was cured.

After Mr. Right had been flying and continuing his regular injections for about three months, a newspaper article appeared, claiming that Krebiozen was not as effective as had originally been thought. Mr. Right called the hospital in a panic and asked his doctor, "What's going on here?" His doctor said, "I don't know. I'll have to call the makers of Krebiozen and find out." Within a week Mr. Right's tumors had reformed and he was back in the hospital on oxygen once again.

Then his doctor thought, "I'm going to try something which under normal circumstances I would never try." He told Mr. Right that he had obtained a supply of new, improved Krebiozen, that the old Krebiozen hadn't worked because of a short shelf life. And he began to give Mr. Right injections of distilled water. As he did that, Mr. Right's tumors melted like a snowball on a hot stove. Within a month he was out of the hospital and back flying his private plane.

Open Loop No.5

Now, one of my favourite stories is that one day a very young Milton Erickson was walking down the street in the town where he lived, and he heard from over there somewhere a noise. And he said, "I think *there's something to learn here.*" So he looked in the direction of the noise, and he saw a building and a large sign on top of the building that said "Boiler Factory." So he went across the street, and opened a door. He could feel the tug of the door in his hand as he stepped over the threshold, and then he went inside. And when he got inside, the noise was tremendous. And he could see the workers, and they were all moving purposefully back and forth inside this boiler factory, but he couldn't hear them. I don't know if you know this, but in those days, they used to make *big* boilers. Imagine a boiler the size of this room. *Can you?* A boiler the size of this room, with sheets of steel, maybe an inch or two thick, and rivets along the top, and maybe there would be *one rivet every two feet, or two rivets every 18 inches, or maybe 3 rivets every foot,* along the top, and then rivets along the ends, sealing in the ends. If you could imagine being in a boiler like that. Those were the kind of boilers they were making in this boiler factory. And so, when he got inside, Erickson said, "There's got to be something to learn here, because these people are communicating inside, and I can't hear them, but they can hear each other." But Erickson couldn't hear them inside. *That's right.* And so, he said, "I've got to learn something about this". So he stopped one of the workers and said, "Can you get me the Boss? Ask the boss to come outside so I can speak to him." The first worker he asked didn't know what to do, so he asked another worker, "Can you get me the boss? Can you ask the Boss to come outside so we can have a discussion?" The boss came outside and Erickson said, "I'd like to sleep here for the evening. I'm a student and I'm learning how to communicate inside a boiler factory". Now in those days, I guess it was all right, because the Boss said OK. So Erickson went home and got his pillow and his blanket and he went back into the boiler factory, and he went across the steps and pulled the door open and once again, all of a sudden, there was all this noise inside… from the workers going back and forth, the sheets of steel moving on the conveyers, and the riveters riveting. He said, "For the life of me, I almost can't *hear myself think*." But he managed to *find a place out of the way*. So he laid out his pillow and his blanket and got under the blanket…snuggled up…but even so the noise was inside his head…loud as ever. But about midnight, he managed to *take all the noise and put it outside* his head, and then he fell asleep. *Very good.*

Erickson was always putting himself in situations like that. Situations where he could *learn. That's right.* About what happens inside you. Not your Conscious Mind, *your Unconscious*…and really Unconscious…and *you don't mind, do you?*

Marginal Note:

Metaphors are the gentlest, most elegant way to begin talking directly with your client's Unconscious Mind. They can be stories from your own experience or someone else's (or no one's). They can sound realistic or mythical. They can be true stories, or stories invented specifically for your client's situation.

Have you noticed that in front of an audience a professional speaker almost always begins with a metaphor? The speaker's metaphor is often a joke, but sometimes a dramatic story to introduce their subject. Speakers may or may not know *why* a metaphor is the best opening… they may or may not realize that they are hooking the attention of the Unconscious Minds of their audiences. But they know that metaphors *work*.

The content of a well-selected metaphor will relate to something in the client's (or the audience's) experience. The process of noticing the parallels is part of what triggers the Unconscious Mind's curiosity and opens it to dialogue. And the ultimate aim of the metaphor is to awaken in the listener a specifically targeted mental state… very often the state that the character experiences in the metaphor.

The language of a well-told metaphor will be deliciously ambiguous, utilizing Milton Model patterns freely to further feed the curiosity of the client's Unconscious Mind.

In planning a hypnotherapy session, Erickson would review his notes about the patient's presenting problem and personal history, and then choose or invent several suitable metaphors. In conducting the session, he would open a 'loop' by starting the first metaphor and telling three-quarters or more of it. Then he would break off that story and open another loop by starting the second metaphor, then break off the second and start the third. He often used as many as four or five metaphors. This served as an elegant way to do a trance induction without making any specific reference to hypnosis!

Leaving the metaphors incomplete, that is, leaving the loops open, excited the curiosity of his patient's Unconscious Mind. When Erickson observed that the opening of several loops had put him in direct communication with the patient's Unconscious, he would then proceed with the change work which was the purpose of the session. When he had completed the change work, he would 'close' the most recently opened loop by telling the end of the metaphor, and go on to close all of the loops in the reverse order to which he had opened them. The effect of closing the metaphors was to lead the patient out of the trance. Because Erickson chose metaphors very carefully, a second effect was that the story endings reinforced the change work done while the patient was in trance.

Critical to the effectiveness of Erickson's metaphors were the 'break points' in the stories. A well-chosen break would interrupt the story and leave a loop open at a point of peak interest, with a sense of incompletion engaging the curiosity of the patient's Unconscious for the dialogue that was to follow. The closing of the loop at the end would satisfy the curiosity of the Unconscious and reinforce the change work.

Before the end of this chapter, I will be recommending that you experiment with Erickson's method of choosing a series of metaphors to lead a client into trance and, after accomplishing intended change work, lead them back out of it.

Close Loop No.5

When Milton Erickson awoke the next morning inside the boiler factory, the first thing he heard was the workers saying, "What does that kid think he can *learn here*, when it has taken us so long to *learn how to communicate inside*?" But he knew that he'd learned something very valuable. He knew he'd learned something that could carry him through his entire life. He knew because if you can *communicate with your Unconscious…* your Unconscious Mind, you can *ask it to do anything. Clear up your health, have you be happy, find the way to realize your deepest desires.* Just communicating with your Unconscious Mind. At least that's what Erickson thought. What do you think?

Close Loop No.4

Six months after Mr. Right's second release from the hospital, the American Medical Association made the final announcement that Krebiozen was totally worthless in the treatment of cancer. Within three days, Mr. Right returned to the hospital and died.

What is important about this story is the healing power you have inside your own body. I first told this story at an NLP Practitioner Training. One woman in the class had a dramatic reaction to hearing the story. Within a week, a lump she had had in her breast disappeared. The power that you have to heal is very, very important.

Close Loop No.3

And back in the Dean's office, the Professor said, "John, since you knew all 10 questions and the order they were in, I believe *you know the answers*. And the Dean said, "I'm going to recommend that *you get an A in this course*." In fact, Erickson said that John got all A's because he knew how to *pay attention to everything*. He really knew how to *look at people and listen to them*, and he knew that that was a learning he would remember the rest of his life. And *he did*.

Close Loop No.2

I never got caught looking at Christmas presents. I *never did*, I really never did. But they always *knew*. And now that you're a parent, *don't you know*? There's that little telltale sign, of the slightly ripped paper, and you say, "I guess I'd better change my hiding place next year." But all the while, that curiosity: Hey, what's going on in there? What's happening? Inside?

Close Loop No.1

And as you continue to *LEARN HYPNOSIS EASILY AND EFFORT-LESSLY*, you may not need to *develop those 30 pages that Erickson did*. You can *rely on his experience* to *talk less and less, and observe and utilize more.*

And I can assure you that the more you really *pay attention to detail*, the richer your experience will be as you *lead your clients easily into trance and talk with their Unconscious Minds.*

A Practical Exercise in Creating Metaphors

If you had *heard* the previous section on "Multiple Embedded Metaphors" instead of reading it, you would probably have experienced metaphor-induced trance. The change work that I chose to sandwich between the multiple loop openings and the reverse order closings was a learning experience rather than the type of personal change that would be more usual for a hypnotherapy session.

I invite you to take some time now to plan a similar series of five multiple embedded metaphors. First choose a colleague to whom you will tell the metaphors. (With a specific person in mind, you can design the metaphors to have the effects you intend for that person.) Think of five stories, 2 to 4 minutes each. Think of what the effects will be, and organize the stories in the best order. Prepare the stories in your mind, so that you can begin each one, tell 80 or 90% of it, and then stop and go on to the next story.

In choosing the content of your metaphors, consider:

- stories about people learning things
- stories about connections people made inside
- stories of understandings people reached
- stories that had certain effects on people
- stories of revelations people had.

As you think about a story you may use, imagine the effect it would have on your colleague hearing that story for the first time.

Think of where you can break the stories, and where you will pick them up again as you conclude. Plan to sandwich your content, or change work, in the middle.

To prepare for practising these metaphors with your colleague, plan as your central content some useful suggestions about learning or about unlocking the power of the Unconscious Mind.

For your convenience in planning metaphors, copy the diagram on page 125.

Once you have your metaphors and central content planned, practise them with your colleague acting as the client. Practise several times, observing the effects of your stories and your choices of where to break each metaphor. Use your observations to improve the flow and the effects of your multiple embedded metaphors until you are delighted with the results.

Hypnotic Language Patterns

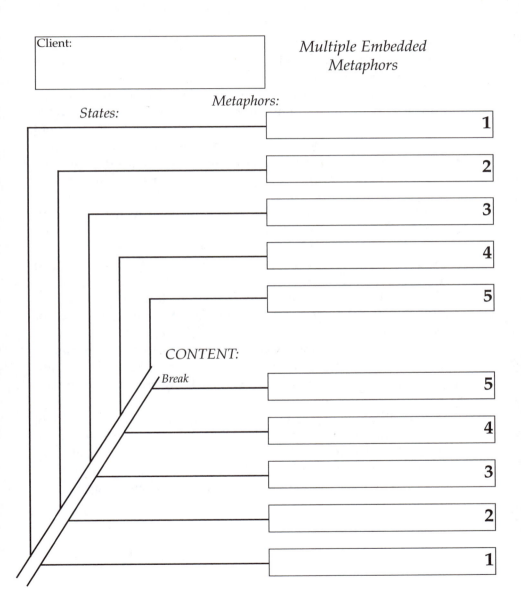

Refining Your Style for Working with Metaphors

Erickson often took as long as a week to design a hypnotic intervention for a patient. He took great care in planning the metaphors that he would use.

As you begin to experiment with creating metaphors, I recommend two good sources: *Therapeutic Metaphors* by David Gordon, and *The Answer Within* by Lankton and Lankton. There are also a number of good courses on metaphors in the American Institute of Hypnotherapy's doctorate programme. You will get excellent results from a careful study of how to design metaphors and predict their effects. The best teacher, however, will be your own experience and experiments as you create and use metaphors.

Do not limit yourself to stories that you have heard or experienced. You can create stories from scratch that will exactly address the needs of your clients. One of Erickson's famous stories is a deep level metaphor about tomatoes. To a client who wanted to lose weight he said, "You know, I'm growing some tomatoes in my backyard. And the interesting thing about the tomatoes is that they know what to eat to be the right size. Tomatoes always come out to be just the size they're supposed to be." And he continued with a long, involved metaphor of how a tomato pulls the nutrients up from the soil, taking in the right amount of water and the right amount of nutrients. That is one way of doing an intervention!

As you continue to experiment with metaphors, you will find new ways not only to use them in inducing trance, but also to weave them into the change work that you do when the client is already in trance. And your subtlety and effectiveness will grow. People love stories. The Unconscious Mind is intrigued by metaphors.

Chapter 14

Progressive Test Induction
Based on Estabrooks

Up to this point we have focused on Erickson's indirect, permissive approach. It is easy to learn and comfortable to use with most clients, including those who may have some hesitations about being hypnotized. We will now examine reasons for sometimes using the more traditional approach to hypnotism... a direct, authoritarian approach.

One of the advantages of traditional hypnotism is its usefulness for producing deep trance phenomena. Even Ericksonian hypnotists usually move toward a more authoritarian approach when they need to induce deep trance to elicit the deeper hypnotic phenomena.

Most hypnotherapy today is done in an Ericksonian style, with the client in a waking state. In traditional hypnotism, on the other hand, the hypnotist talks about sleep at the beginning of the induction and leads the client into a sleeping state. This is useful especially in getting the client to forget what happens during trance. If the desired outcome is, say, for the client to stop smoking or have an aversion to certain fattening foods, post-hypnotic suggestions will work best when the client forgets the suggestions; their Conscious Mind will then not interfere with their carrying out the suggestions.

One of this century's greatest teachers of the traditional approach was George Estabrooks, a professor at Colgate University, whose book *Hypnotism* was published in 1943. Estabrooks taught a direct, authoritarian approach. If we were to begin this chapter's induction in his style, it would sound like this: "Close your eyes. You are falling asleep—sound asleep. Relax all your muscles and imagine that you are going into a deep sleep. Deeper and deeper and deeper. You will not wake up until I tell you... then you will wake up quietly and you will feel fine as a result of these suggestions. You are falling sound, sound asleep. Deeper and deeper and deeper." For your later reference, a complete induction in Estabrooks's direct, authoritative style appears in the appendix.

For ease in learning and practising, we will use an induction based on Estabrooks's style and adapted by the addition of Ericksonian indirect suggestions.

I call this a Progressive Test Induction. I recommend that you practise it with a colleague, taking turns as Hypnotherapist and client. The induction will take the client through all six stages of hypnosis discussed in Chapter 8. Each step the client reaches will be a further successful test of his ability to hypnotize himself. In other words, the client's success in reaching each stage will act as a strong convincer, so that the further into the induction you get, the stronger the client's belief will become that they are a great hypnotic subject... the more they will lead themself inward... and the more accepting they will become of your suggestions.

After each test, you will lead the client to once again relax the part of their body that was involved in that test.

Each client is different. Sometimes a client will not succeed at a certain level of this induction, and will then succeed very readily at deeper levels. If, after a reasonable amount of suggestion, the client does not produce the trance phenomenon you expect at one of the levels, utilize whatever the client does instead, and move on to the next level.

When the client has reached a deep level of trance, make post-hypnotic suggestions that will be of benefit to them after the induction, and produce amnesia of those suggestions. Before you bring the client out of trance, the script will prompt you to *remove* any *test* suggestions that the client should not continue to follow when the induction is finished.

As you use the script below, repeat or expand on sentences as needed, in order to maintain a smooth flow and assist the client into total relaxation.

Progressive Test Induction Adapted from Estabrooks

Close Eyes – Talk Sleep

> Now, if you would like to just go ahead and see if you can close your eyes. And I wonder if you can imagine, everybody can, imagining is something you can do, remember how much you imagined when you were little, or you can

just remember a time when you were falling asleep (*yawn*), just falling sound asleep. Now, perhaps you can remember a time when you were soo-oo tired, and relaxed… all your muscles totally… relax… and just remember a time when you were falling asleep, going into a deep sleep. Deeper and deeper and deeper… (*etc*). That's right. Now, this is important, you can stay asleep as long as you want to stay asleep until I tell you, and remember, you will always hear the sound of my voice, however far or deep you go and you will always feel just fine and be just fine as a result of these suggestions. So, it's OK, just go ahead and fall sound, sound asleep. Deeper and deeper and deeper asleep. (*Continue talking this way for 5 minutes.*) You may or may not remember to forget everything that happens. It's OK.

Eyelids Locked Closed

Now, listen. As deeply relaxed as you are, you still know your eyes are closed, and you may not have noticed that your eyelids feel so heavy that they are, and they really ARE locked so tightly together that you may find it quite amusing to discover that your eyes are locked tight, tight, tightly together. That's right. Your eyelids are locked tightly together and you cannot open your eyes no matter how hard you try, and REALLY try, the tighter they become. And you might care to try, so go ahead, I dare you to try and find with some amusement that you cannot.

Relaxation. Now relax everything. Relax your eyelids. They are returning to normal, and you are sound asleep. Sound, sound asleep, and you will sleep until I tell you. Then you will awaken quietly and easily… until then, just relax everything and sleep, sleep, sleep.

Stiff Arm

Now it's time for our next test. So just notice your right arm, right where it is (*describe*) is becoming stiff and rigid, rigid and stiff. Stiff and rigid. And everyone knows how a piece of iron feels, so rigid and stiff, just like you… cannot bend your right arm. It's just like an iron bar, solid, rigid, and stiff. It is impossible to bend your right arm's so stiff. I dare you to discover with some amusement you cannot. That's right.

Relaxation. Now relax everything. Relax your right arm. It is returning to normal, and you are sound asleep. Sound, sound asleep, and you will sleep until I tell you. Then you will awaken quietly and easily… until then, just relax everything and sleep, sleep, sleep.

Weak Legs

Now, even though you never thought of this before, now notice it's as if your body is floating away, floating away, floating away. And you may discover with some delight that you cannot control the muscles in your legs, you are so relaxed now. And where were you born? Do you remember? (*The purpose of these questions is to induce an age regression, taking the client back to a time when the motor movements in their legs were not yet developed.*) Remember! Being a little newborn baby…. And now, like then, you're stuck where you are, and your legs won't work, too relaxed. That's right. It is impossible for you to even try to stand up, too relaxed. And the harder you may try, the more relaxed your legs. You are just stuck there in the chair. You may try, and really try, I dare you.

Relaxation. Now relax everything. Relax your legs. They are returning to normal, and you are sound asleep. Sound, sound asleep, and you will sleep until I tell you. Then you will awaken quietly and easily… until then, just relax everything and sleep, sleep, sleep.

Automatic Movement

Now listen carefully, more fun. It's time for us to discover just what your hands can do. In a moment, I'm going to

132

touch your hands. (*When the client's eyes are closed, always tell them you are going to touch them before you do. Use ambiguous touch to establish catalepsy in one arm, then the other.*) Now, let's start your hands rotating. Here they go. (*Start the hands rotating.*) Here they go, round and around. Faster and faster. Can your Unconscious... keep them moving? That's right. They ARE rotating faster and faster. And you just might find with some delight you cannot stop them. You cannot stop, no matter how hard you try, the harder you try, the faster they go around and around.

Relaxation. Now relax everything. (*Gently hold the hands to stop the rotating.*) Relax your hands. They are returning to rest on your lap, and you are sound asleep. Sound, sound asleep, and you will sleep until I tell you. Then you will awaken quietly and easily... until then, just relax everything and sleep, sleep, sleep.

Talking in Your Sleep

Now I want you to dream, and REALLY dream of talking in your sleep. Everyone knows of someone who talks in their sleep. So sleep and have that dream. Now I am going to ask you a few simple questions, and you can just remain asleep in your dream, and dream you answer me in your sleep, talking in your sleep as you have seen other people talk in their sleep. Soon I'm going to ask questions you will find it easy to answer... here they are:

What is your name?   (*Wait for an answer, possibly repeat the question.*)
What is your address?

Relaxation. Now relax everything. Your voice is again silent and you are sound asleep. Sound, sound asleep, and you will sleep until I tell you. Then you will awaken quietly and easily... until then, just relax everything and sleep, sleep, sleep.

Sleep Walking

Now in a moment you will stand up. I will help you. You will remain asleep as you stand up, as if you were in a dream. You have seen sleepwalkers. Finding it easy to stand up. Now I'm going to touch you, to help you. (*Help client.*) Go ahead, stand up. Walk. That's right. You are finding it easy to use your leg muscles as you remain deeply asleep. Standing up. And as you sit down (*help client*), go even more deeply asleep. You can sit down safely and comfortably.

Relaxation. Now relax everything. Relax your legs. They are returning to normal, and you are sound asleep. Sound, sound asleep, and you will sleep until I tell you. Then you will awaken quietly and easily... until then, just relax everything and sleep, sleep, sleep.

Visual Hallucinations

Now listen carefully. In a moment you're going to awaken from the neck up only. Your mind can remain asleep, and your body can remain asleep, but just your head, with no recognition of your body, can awaken from the neck up. When you're ready, just open your eyes. Open them now, and remain deeply asleep. You are still dreaming, and I want you to dream of this tennis ball. Open your eyes and look at the tennis ball in my hand. What color is it? (*Hold up hand as if holding tennis ball in it. Toss the ball up. See if client follows the ball.*) Now I'm going to turn the ball a little bit so you can see the number on it. Once you've got the color and the number, you can close your eyes, staying deeply, deeply asleep.

Relaxation. Now relax everything. Your eyes are returning to normal, and you are sound asleep. Sound, sound asleep, and you will sleep until I tell you. Then you will awaken quietly and easily... until then, just relax everything and sleep, sleep, sleep.

NOTE: For demonstration purposes, **Full Body Catalepsy** can be added to the Progressive Test Induction at this point. For details, see the Appendix, page 188. Full Body Catalepsy is not included here in the text because extreme care is needed in inducing it, and it is more commonly done in the training of Hypnotherapists than in actual therapy.

Insert Post-Hypnotic Suggestions

Now in a moment I am going to give your Unconscious Mind some suggestions, which I would like your Conscious Mind to forget. Forgetting is normal and natural. Forgetting is a normal, natural thing... you do it all the time. Why would you care what you had for lunch two weeks ago, on Wednesday, when it rained? You simply forget it. I want you to forget consciously what I am about to tell you in just a moment. Somebody gives you a slip of paper and you forget about it. Where did it go? Who knows, who cares, just forget about it. Forgetting is a normal, natural thing. Now, I would like to suggest that.... (*Make suitable positive suggestions related to learning, the supplying of needed information by the Unconscious Mind, or a topic of your choosing. At this point, the suggestions should be direct!*) And I want you to forget my suggestions consciously and remember them unconsciously... like the piece of paper you've forgotten about... like who cares what you had for lunch two weeks ago. It's OK, forgetting's a normal, natural thing. Forget what I just said.

Clear the Test or Short-Term Suggestions

Now with your eyes closed, stay deeply asleep for a little while longer. All suggestions I have given you about this trance and all related tests are now removed. All ongoing suggestions are still in effect. (*The client can differentiate between the two. He will keep your post-hypnotic suggestions and let go of trance test suggestions.*)

Bring the Client out of Trance

> Now when you are ready, begin to come back. In a moment, I am going to count backwards from 10 to 1, and I want you to awaken one tenth of the way with each number until you are fully awake. 10... 9... 8... etc.

> Practise this Progressive Test Induction with a partner until the talk flows smoothly and effortlessly for you. The induction is a wonderful convincer for the client because it leads them to experience several levels of hypnosis. Likewise, it is rewarding for the new Hypnotherapist to lead the client to those levels.

Further Notes on Progressive Test Induction

Some clients may want to whiz on by any desire to stand up or see a tennis ball, and go quickly as deep as the comatose state. Instead of 'playing silly hypnotic phenomena games,' they may want to go straight to experiencing a deep level of trance. That is fine, as long as they are actualizing what they want in hypnosis. Erickson said that some clients cannot actualize arm levitation in deep trance because they are in a state where they don't care.

The optimum level of trance for making post-hypnotic suggestions varies with each client. You may need to experiment with a client to find the level at which they respond best to suggestion. Erickson would give suggestions to some clients in light trance. He would tell them a few stories, sometimes without doing a formal induction, and they would miraculously change. The key is to establish communication with your client's Unconscious Mind, whether you are using the pendulum or deep trance. Be cautious when you lead a client into deep trance. In some cases, if the client is too deep, they may become unresponsive. If your client goes into a comatose state, you are not going to get the responses you need from them.

For any of the tests in the Progressive Test Induction, the client needs to exert a certain amount of energy. If the client is so relaxed that they cannot do anything further and you want to continue with some of the tests, you can say, "I'd like to ask your Unconscious Mind to send energy to the parts of the body that need energy for this process. Now begin to do this while you stay in a deep trance."

The Progressive Test Induction contains a blend of permissive and authoritarian approaches. I do not recommend a purely direct, authoritarian approach unless you have a client who responds well to it, such as a person with military background or a strictly disciplined upbringing. You can readily begin with a permissive approach and shade into a more authoritarian style as the client progresses deeper into trance.... At deeper levels most Unconscious Minds respond well to authoritarian messages.

The principle of utilization, most closely connected with Erickson's indirect, permissive style, is likewise effective with an authoritarian approach. Utilization can turn what might have been a distraction into a support for the trance induction. It is optimal to notice possible distractions before the client does. You might then say, for example, "In a moment, you may hear a sound coming from outside the room. And you will know that someone is rushing to go somewhere. Perhaps some time in your life, you have rushed to go places. As you notice someone outside rushing to go somewhere, perhaps you will want to go more deeply inside. And take all the time you need, to go even deeper." Utilizing whatever happens outside will help you achieve a smooth, seamless induction. Utilization is hypnosis in all its elegance.

From the standpoint of therapy, the most critical part of the Progressive Test Induction is the insertion of post-hypnotic suggestions at a deep level of trance. The next chapter gives more detail on post-hypnotic suggestions and techniques for deepening trance.

Chapter 15

*Deepening Techniques and
Post-Hypnotic Suggestions*

For a post-hypnotic suggestion to take hold in the client's Unconscious Mind and be forgotten consciously, the client must be in a medium to deep trance when the suggestion is made. The Progressive Test Induction in the previous chapter will take most clients to a fairly deep level, because any suggestions that successfully produce trance phenomena will of their own accord deepen the trance and increase the client's responsiveness. Each successive trance phenomenon acts as a convincer.

Deepening Techniques

Whatever style of induction you are using, there are several techniques that will assist you in leading your client deeper into trance. The first is **direct or indirect suggestion**.

Your suggestion may be connected with a physical cue: "Each time I touch your forehead, notice that you can go even deeper. (*Touch forehead.*) Go even deeper now." Or it may be connected with the client's own physiology: "With every breath you take, you may find a sense of the deepening relaxation that can take you deeper into trance."

Your suggestion can take the form of a deepening image: "Can you imagine walking down a long stairway, going ten floors down, with ten steps for each floor, and as you do, go deep in trance. With each step you take, go deeper. Step 1... 2... 3... 4... 5... 6... 7... 8... 9... 10... and now you are at the first landing on your way down... deep down. And now again, Step 1... 2... etc." To take your client down in comfort and style, you could decide to use an escalator or an elevator.

In Chapter 13, we discussed using **embedded metaphors** to lead a client into trance. Embedded metaphors can also be used to deepen a trance that has already begun. The more levels of metaphor you embed, the deeper the trance will become. (There seems to be a point of diminishing returns after 12 or so embedded metaphors.)

The most profound way to deepen trance is by **repeated induction**. In very early research on hypnotism in the late 1900s,

Hippolyte Bernheim found that when a client reached a certain level of trance during the first visit, they would go to a deeper level when they came back the next week, and a still deeper level during the third visit (*Suggestive Therapeutics*, 1889). His observation was that the more often a client was hypnotized, the deeper they would go.

Erickson and Elman later pointed out that the repeated inductions do not need to be spread over a series of separate sessions. Within one session, they could lead the client to a very deep level by taking them into and out of trance repeatedly, achieving a deeper level each time. The process of achieving deeper levels through repeated inductions is called *fractionation*.

Live Demonstration of Deepening Techniques

As an example of fractionation, here is a transcript of part of a demonstration I did in a class on hypnosis. In addition to the use of repeated inductions for deepening, notice my utilization of the subject's responses.

> (*Chris comes to front of room in response to a gesture that I installed earlier as the trigger for a post-hypnotic suggestion to do that. Current theory holds that when a post-hypnotic suggestion activates, a client goes back into the same trance they were in when the suggestion was made.*)
>
> **Tad**:   Have a seat please, Chris. Are you in a trance right now?
>
> **Chris**: I don't know.
>
> **Tad**:   That's right, you don't know. Good. Not knowing is a good thing in hypnosis; you know that, don't you? Why don't you close your eyes, if you'd like, and go really, really deeply in trance. You know how to do this, just go really deeply in trance. Just go very, very deeply asleep. Deeper and deeper in trance, just go even deeper. In a moment, Chris,

I'm going to touch you on the shoulder. When I touch you on the shoulder, I would like you to double your relaxation...when I touch you on the shoulder (*touching*), right now. OK, that's good. Now go even deeper, Chris. I am going to ask you once again to double your relaxation, when I touch you on the shoulder...right now. Just double your relaxation, go even deeper, go even deeper.... OK, Chris, remembering where you are, why don't you come on back. Good, now you're back.

(*Taking Chris back into trance again.*) Now I would like you to go right back to where you were, and double your relaxation from there. Just double your relaxation and go even deeper. That's right. Even more deeply asleep.

OK, Chris, once again open your eyes, please. You're doing great. Are you in a trance now?

Chris: I don't know.

Tad: Not knowing is perfect, you know?

Chris: Well... I think so.

Tad: You do think so. Let me ask you something. (*Referring to visual hallucination step in earlier induction.*) Before when I showed you the tennis ball, what color was it?

Chris: I didn't see it.

Tad: You didn't see it. Would you like to see it?

Chris: Yes, I would.

Tad: You would like to. So let's ask your Unconscious Mind to assist you in developing whatever you need to develop to be able to see the tennis ball. This time when you close your eyes and go deeply asleep... and I will assist you by touching you on

143

the shoulder and you can double your relaxation again from where you were. Then I would like you to ask your Unconscious Mind to just develop whatever inner mechanisms or imagination you need, so that you can see something. And if you don't see it clearly the first time, then perhaps you could see what you *would* see, if you could see it. You see? Good. Just go ahead and close your eyes and go even more deeply asleep, good. Just go very deeply asleep, that's right. Deeper now, deeper, just relax every single muscle. Double your relaxation again, double it again, and go even deeper. Chris, I'd like you to make sure that the muscles around your eyes are so relaxed that you can't open them. And when you know they are, go ahead and test them, and notice how they stay totally closed. Good. Remaining deeply asleep, I'd like to borrow both your hands for a moment. I am just going to simply see what happens if we just (*setting hands in motion*)... that's right. Remaining deeply asleep, let your hands remain doing whatever they are doing right now. (*Chris's hands are now automatically rotating.*) Good, Chris, relax those hands. I'd like you to remain deeply asleep. You can awaken by opening your eyes and not your body. Your Conscious Mind can stay asleep, and your Unconscious Mind can awaken from the neck up. When you open your eyes, I am going to pick up this tennis ball from the floor. I am actually going to show you... mmmmm... the tennis ball. Go ahead and open your eyes, and take a peek. What color is that?

Chris: I can't see it.

Tad: That's fine, just close your eyes and fall deeply asleep. Double your relaxation again. Now just ask your Unconscious Mind what needs to happen so that you can see the tennis ball, just go ahead and do that now. And let your Unconscious Mind make the necessary connections for you to be able to see. (*After a pause*) OK, Chris, ask your Unconscious Mind if it has made the necessary connections in your neurology so that you are ready to proceed. When you are ready, open your eyes and notice this tennis ball. See what you could see, if you could see it. That is the first step. Good, what color is the ball?

Chris: Orange.

Tad: Excellent, very good. What's the number on the ball?

Chris: 3.

Tad: I am going to toss the tennis ball over to your chair and you can keep it, if you'd like. I'll just throw it over there now.... Good, Chris.... Go ahead and close your eyes and double your relaxation once more, go even deeper.

In this demonstration, I asked Chris to develop the necessary faculties to have a positive hallucination. If the client has not produced a hypnotic phenomenon that we are looking for at a deeper level, we can assist them in doing that. Having the client go in and out of trance is perfect. While they are in trance, we can give them suggestions to modify their neurology, or to have whatever changes are needed occur inside, so that they will be able to actualize a phenomenon that previously they could not.

Some people need extra work on their neurological connections to be able to positively hallucinate an object. Others can do this very readily. These people have a skill common to architects. Architects get paid for their hallucinations. They earn six-figure incomes for hallucinating buildings where there are none.

A person who can hallucinate a tennis ball can visualize the healing of a diseased part of their body. Chris learned something very valuable in the demonstration. He went through the first stages of teaching himself how to positively hallucinate something. This will serve him very well in the future in terms of imagining his body healing itself and being whole.

Techniques for Making Post-Hypnotic Suggestions

Post-hypnotic suggestions are imperative to successful change work in hypnosis. A post-hypnotic suggestion is a suggestion that activates and operates at a time... or times... after the client has come out of trance. Typically, the client will feel a compelling desire to respond, often without remembering or realizing what has prompted the desire.

To make your post-hypnotic suggestions effective, remember the following points:

- **Lead the client into medium to deep trance** in order to produce amnesia for the suggestion, which is usually desirable so that the Conscious Mind will not interfere with the working of the suggestion. (In some cases the post-hypnotic suggestion can work even if the client remembers it. Some people later remember a suggestion when they are in trance and not when they are out of trance.)

- Any suggestions given while the client is in deep trance should be **clear and to the point**. Early in the induction, while the client is in a waking state, indirect suggestions are effective. Later, when the client is in deep trance, make your post-hypnotic suggestions direct and authoritarian. (This was pointed out by Boris Sidis in *The Psychology of Suggestion*, 1898.)

- **Keep your talk congruent with what you are really thinking**. The Unconscious Mind is amazingly perceptive, and can readily detect incongruities between what you are telling it and the messages given by your voice and physiology. Think what you want the client to do as you are asking them to do it. Remember, your client will only actualize those things that you believe to be true.

- **Embed the suggestion in multiple metaphors**. This technique is distinctly Ericksonian. Remember the metaphors in the Progressive Test Induction: "Now in a moment I am going to give your Unconscious Mind some suggestions, which I would like your Conscious Mind to forget. Forgetting is normal and natural. Forgetting is a normal, natural thing... you do it all the time. Why would you care what you had for lunch two weeks ago, on Wednesday, when it rained? You simply forget it. I want you to forget consciously what I am about to tell you in just a moment. Somebody gives you a slip of paper and you forget about it. Where did it go? Who knows, who cares, just forget about it. Forgetting is a normal, natural thing. Now, I would like to suggest that...."

- **Tell the client what the trigger will be** to set off the activation of the post-hypnotic suggestion. If I myself am going to trigger activation of a suggestion during a classroom demonstration, I tell the subject that when they see me rub my hand across my upper lip, they will, for example, walk up to the front of the room.

- **Tell the client clearly what to do**. Example: "You will feel an undeniable urge to stand up, and you will stand up and walk to the front of the room." Then tell the client **when to do it**. Example: "You will do this immediately."

- **Close the metaphor loops:** "And I want you to forget my suggestions consciously and remember them unconsciously... like the piece of paper you've forgotten about... like who cares what you had for lunch two weeks ago. It's OK, forgetting is a normal, natural thing. Forget what I just said."

In stage hypnosis and classroom demonstrations, post-hypnotic suggestions are designed to be activated just after the client has come out of trance, by the signal the hypnotist has set as a trigger. In therapy, post-hypnotic suggestions are set to be activated repeatedly over a long period, sometimes in response to an external trigger, or very often in response to some internal trigger in the client's own behaviour.

Here is an example of suggestions that you might make to a colleague in practising post-hypnotic suggestions for the purpose of therapy:

I know that you want to be an excellent Hypnotherapist. And now I want to ask your Unconscious Mind to organize everything that you've been studying, everything that you've heard experienced Hypnotherapists say, all of the examples of things to say to your clients. And you can remember those things, and your Unconscious Mind can present them to your Conscious Mind in such a way that you don't even have to think about them.

When you are listening to a client, your complete attention will be on what the client is saying, riveted, because you know that when it is time for you to respond, your Unconscious Mind will immediately supply the response that will most help the client.

And when you are talking to a client and searching for the next thing to say, you will relax and pause quietly, because you know that your Unconscious Mind is about to give you the best thing to say. Just relax. Your Unconscious Mind will organize everything you have learned about hypnosis and will easily and effortlessly supply the things that you need to say in order to have your clients go into deep trance and experience the most excellent results from the hypnotherapy process.

That would be all right, wouldn't it? Just nod "Yes" when your Unconscious Mind has organized all your learnings about hypnosis. That's right. Excellent.

Post-hypnotic suggestions can last for as short or as long a time as you suggest. You can specify that a suggestion will last only for a single occasion. You can make a deeply beneficial suggestion that will last forever.

Chapter 16

Elman Methods

Dave Elman was one of the first people to propose that all hypnosis is self hypnosis. In his book *Hypnotherapy* in 1964, Elman said,

> "I have been teaching hypnosis... for years, and have found that many [people] seem to think that they can become expert hypnotists after a few classroom and practice sessions. Since there is really no such thing as a hypnotist, this is obviously impossible. As a practitioner employing this tool, all you can ever do is show a patient how to go over the hurdle from a normal waking or sleeping state into that peculiar state of mind known as hypnosis. You won't hypnotize them; they will hypnotize themselves. This means that all of us using suggestion wield no 'power' over any subject. It means that there is nothing that I can do that you can't learn to do in hypnosis."

Elman was born in Fargo, North Dakota in 1890. His father did stage hypnosis and owned a general store in North Dakota, where he kept a collection of books on hypnosis. Dave Elman mastered these books. He learned hypnosis so well that he had to drop it for a while when he went off to school, because it scared some of his classmates. In his later years Elman taught hypnosis to medical doctors.

Dave Elman proposed a model of hypnosis that was clearly different from earlier models. In watching his father perform, Elman noticed that a stage hypnotist had to put people in trance a lot more quickly than a Hypnotherapist, in the interests of showmanship. He was fascinated by the ability of a stage hypnotist to hypnotize a large group in a short time. And the trances his father induced were deep enough to produce hypnotic phenomena very quickly. Elman developed a method of hypnosis that would produce a deep trance as quickly as possible.

To better understand what is different about Elman's method, let us compare it with other methods we have discussed. Traditional hypnosis is generally authoritarian, using a direct induction to achieve a sleeping trance. Ericksonian hypnosis is permissive and indirect, leading more often to waking trance than to sleeping. Neuro Linguistic Programming interventions (which are a strong resource for a hypnotherapist) are authoritarian and indirect, with the client almost always in a waking state.

Elman techniques do not fit any of these models. His inductions could be authoritarian or permissive, direct or indirect, leading to waking or sleeping trance! The chart below summarizes these differences.

Type of Hypnosis	*Approach to Client*	*Style of Induction*	*Type of Trance*
Traditional Hypnosis	Authoritarian	Direct	Sleeping
Ericksonian Hypnosis	Permissive	Indirect	Waking or Sleeping
NLP Intervention	Authoritarian	Indirect	Waking
Elman's Hypnosis	Authoritarian or Permissive	Direct or Indirect	Waking or Sleeping

The greatest defining characteristic of Elman's technique is that it induces trance almost instantaneously by setting up a dissociation between the Conscious and Unconscious Minds. The hypnotist is thus able to speak more directly with the Unconscious Mind, with minimal filtering by the Conscious. In Elman hypnosis, the therapist says, "Close your eyes and pretend you can't open them, knowing full well that you can." According to Elman, creating that paradox at once sets up the conditions in which hypnosis can occur.

Elman's second principal innovation was to give the client the responsibility for going into trance. He said, "When a person rejects hypnosis, it simply means he has refused *to bypass his critical faculty* and [so has made] the *implanting of selective thinking impossible.* It doesn't mean he can't be hypnotized or won't be hypnotized, but simply that he refused to follow instructions. If he does follow properly given instructions, hypnosis is possible for him just as it is for everyone." (Italics added.)

In other words, the percentage of people who can be hypnotized is one hundred per cent. Elman says that everyone can be hypnotized and everyone can achieve a deep level of trance easily, if they *follow instructions.*

Elman also had a resourceful approach to obtaining eye closure:

"Practically all textbooks declare that you must first obtain eye closure if you wish to obtain hypnosis, and that eye closure can usually be obtained by the methods called fixation, monotony, rhythm, imitation or levitation. I will obtain eye closure without these methods. 'Close your eyes and pretend you can't open them. Keep on pretending, and while you are pretending, try to open your eyes.' You'll find that it is impossible, if you are concentrating hard on the pretence. Now you know very well that you can open your eyes any time that you change your mind and stop pretending. All the time you were pretending that you could not open your eyes, your sense of judgment was completely suspended concerning that particular action. We obtained the same eye closure we would if we used the techniques of fixation, monotony, rhythm, imitation, or levitation. This can be done instantaneously."

Elman continues:

"But does it mean that you are hypnotized? Indeed it does not. It is merely the entering wedge and hypnosis is not obtained until selective thinking is firmly established. Selective thinking is whatever you believe *wholeheartedly*. For example, if you are led to believe that you will feel no pain, and you believe it completely, you will feel no pain. Let the slightest doubt come in and the selective thinking vanishes; the critical faculty is no longer bypassed.... The introduction of fear causes a defensive reaction that brings the critical faculty back into focus."

Elman's Stages of Hypnosis

In Chapter 8, we discussed LeCron's six stages of hypnosis, ranging over a continuum of light, medium and deep trance. Elman offers a simpler scheme of four levels of trance:

- Light or superficial trance
- Somnambulistic trance

153

- Coma
- Hypnosis attached to sleep.

Conditions for Hypnosis, and Pre-Talk

Dave Elman specifies four pre-requisites for a successful induction.

- First, in order for hypnosis to occur, the subject must agree to be hypnotized.
- Second, there must be communication between the Hypnotherapist and the client.
- Third, the client must be free from any fear about the hypnotic process or what is going to take place.
- And finally, the client must be free from reluctance. The client must trust the Hypnotherapist and their intentions.

The pre-talk ought to set up these conditions. From Elman's point of view, much of the work of hypnosis occurs before the induction. We need to eliminate the client's fears and misconceptions. Here is a sample of pre-talk in the Elman style:

Elman Pre-Talk

Make a fist. Relax.

You know that if you wanted to, you could tighten your muscles and make a fist that was so strong that you couldn't make it any stronger or any more powerful. Isn't that true? So, if you wanted, and if you knew how, you could also make any group of muscles you wanted so absolutely, totally relaxed that unless you removed the relaxation, you could relax those muscles to the point where they wouldn't work. That is also true, isn't it?

Eyelids are the easiest to relax.

The easiest muscles in your entire body to relax are your eyelids. Now, you know that's true, don't you? Remember a time when you were tired, had a rough day, and you closed your eyes, and it just feels so good.

"Now, watch what I do." (*Demonstrate this to the client while you are talking.*)

I'm going to close my eyes, and I am going to relax them so completely and so deeply that if I do not take that relaxation away, they won't work. Nothing that I can do or say or think will make them open. Now I can take away the relaxation and they will open instantly, but if the relaxation is there, they won't work.

"Now I'm going to try to open my eyes." (*Open eyes.*)

Now I tested myself to see that they did work, and I did the wrong thing, because I wanted to test them to be sure they do **not** work.

"This time I am going to keep them shut."

This time I am going to relax my eyelids to the point where they won't work. And I am going to hold on to the relaxation and then test them to make sure they do not work. I don't have to prove they will work, I can do that every day. I know that I can instantly remove the relaxation by the slightest thought, the slightest desire, so I am not going to do that this time. This time I'm going to allow them to stay totally relaxed, and I know that as long as I stay totally relaxed, and as long as I do not take that relaxation away, nothing I can do or say or think will cause them to open. Watch. See, they stay there like an old shoe. And I know it looks stupid with my eyebrows going up and down, but it feels great!

"You can do it too!"

Now, I can feel proud of myself, because I did it. I can take the relaxation away and I can open my eyes. You know, 5-year-old kids can do this; you can do this, too. Just see if you can do what I do. Close your eyes, and put your awareness on your eyelids. You're in charge, you're in control, and your muscles have to do what you tell them to do.

"They respond to what you tell them."

Not what I tell them to do… they respond to you, not me. Your eyelids respond to you because the suggestions are coming directly from you, and through your neurology. You direct your body to follow those suggestions totally and completely, and you will be successful.

Have the client do it.

So, go ahead, tell your body to relax your eyelid muscles totally and completely, so deeply and completely that unless you remove the relaxation, they just won't work. And when you know that you have accomplished this, then hold on to the relaxation and give them a good test, and notice that they stay shut; make sure they won't work, and notice how good that feels. Test them hard, really try. (*If* client opens eyes:) Congratulations; now prove you can relax them so they won't work.

Conclusion

That was the hardest step. You did just great.

Take turns practising this pre-talk with a partner until it flows naturally and smoothly.

Elman Induction No. 1

An Elman induction is a fast, simple progressive test induction, with steps different from the one in Chapter 14. Typically there are six steps for leading the client into deep trance:

*   Deep Breath/Close the Eyes
*   Relax the Eyes
*   Let the relaxation flow through the whole body
*   Open and close the eyes. (*Assist using two fingers. Achieve fractionation by repeating.*)
*   Test for physical relaxation
*   Mental relaxation

If the client does not succeed at a certain level, you re-do that level before going on to the next.

Like Erickson, Elman focused on paying attention to every detail of a client's physical reactions. "True hypnotic signs cannot be aped, imitated or pretended. For example, you cannot pretend body warmth. It has to be there. You cannot imitate fluttering eyelids. Try it for yourself and notice how after a second or two the eyelids no longer flutter. In hypnosis, the fluttering eyelids occur almost constantly as the induction proceeds. There are very few people who can, at will, cause their eyes to tear, nor can you at will cause the whites of your eyes to redden...."

The best way to master the Elman induction is to take turns practising it with a partner. For learning purposes, detailed explanations accompany some of the steps of the induction below. (For later quick reference, the induction is duplicated in the Appendix without explanations.)

When acting as the Hypnotherapist, pay attention to everything the client does, and *utilize*. Any time they do something that seems like trance behaviour, say, *"That's right."*

Be sure that the client follows your instructions exactly. One of the beauties of the Elman Induction is that *it conditions responsiveness to suggestions*. For example, if the client gets ahead of you by closing their eyes before you tell them to, they are *anticipating* your suggestions rather than *responding* to them. This will slow down the induction, making the client less responsive to your suggestions once they are in trance. If the client does something before you instruct them to, go back and repeat, making sure they *follow* your instructions.

Elman Induction No. 1

Take a long, deep breath and hold it for a few seconds.
> (Reminder: if the client closes their eyes when you say, "Take a deep breath," stop the induction and restart. The client needs to do what you say when you say it.)

And as you exhale this breath, allow your eyes to close (Start with your hand above the client's eyes and bring it down to below the chin as the client's eyes are closing), **and let go of the surface tension in your body. Just let your body relax as much as possible, right now.**

Now place your awareness on your eye muscles, and relax the muscles around your eyes to the point where they just won't work. When you're sure they're so relaxed that as long as you hold on to this relaxation they won't work, hold on to that relaxation and test them to make sure THEY WON'T WORK.
> (There are three possibilities:
> * If the client tests and succeeds at keeping their eyes closed, go on to the next step.
> * If they open their eyes, say, "Good, now you've proved you can open your eyes, you've proved you're in charge. You open your eyes every day. Now, prove that you can relax your eyes so much that they'll stay closed."
> * If the client just sits there and doesn't test their eyes, repeat this step; you are conditioning them to respond to your suggestions.)

Now, this relaxation you have in your eyes is the same quality of relaxation that I want you to have throughout your whole body. So let this quality of relaxation flow through your whole body from the top of your head to the tips of your toes.

> (Look for signs of the client becoming much more relaxed as they do this next step.)

> (Each time you tell the client to close their eyes, pass two fingers in front of their face, downward from the forehead to the chin.)

Now we can deepen this relaxation much more. In a moment I'm going to have you open and close your eyes. When you close your eyes, that's your signal to let this feeling of relaxation become ten times deeper. All you have to do is want it to happen, and you can make it happen very easily. OK, now, open your eyes. Now close your eyes (Pass fingers) **and feel that relaxation flowing through your entire body, taking you much deeper. Use your wonderful imagination and imagine your whole body is covered and wrapped in a warm blanket of relaxation.**

> (Again)

Now we can deepen that relaxation much more. In a moment, I'm going to have you open and close your eyes and double the relaxation you have now. Make it become twice as deep. Once more now, open your eyes. Close your eyes (Pass fingers) **and double your relaxation... good. Let every muscle in your body become so relaxed that as long as you hold on to this quality of relaxation, every muscle of your body is totally relaxed.**

> (You are using fractionation to deepen the client's level of trance. Repeat the eye openings and closings until he looks as if you will have to catch him from falling off the chair.)

In a moment, I'm going to have you open and close your eyes once more. Again, when you close your eyes, double the relaxation you now have. Make it twice as deep. Once more, open your eyes... close your eyes and double your relaxation... good. Let every muscle in your body become so relaxed that as long as you hold on to this quality of relaxation, every muscle of your body is totally relaxed.

In a moment (Elman always tells the client what he's going to do before he does it) **I'm going to lift your (right or left) hand by the wrist just a few inches, and drop it. If you have followed my instructions up to this point, that hand will be so relaxed it will be just as loose and limp as a wet dish cloth. It will simply plop down. Now, don't try to help me...you have to remove the realization and let me do all the lifting, so that when I release your hand, it just plops down and you'll allow yourself to go much deeper.** (Lifting hand) **Now the moment your hand plops down on your leg, it will send an even deeper relaxation through your whole body.**

> (Some clients are preconditioned to do arm catalepsy when you lift their hand. That's not what you're looking for, so you may have to talk them through that. If the client helps to lift their hand, say, "Let me do all the lifting, don't help me. Let it be heavy. Don't help me.")

Now, that's complete physical relaxation. I want you to know there are two ways a person can relax. You can relax physically and you can relax mentally. You've already proved that you can relax physically. Now let me show you how to relax mentally.

In a moment, I'll ask you to begin slowly counting backwards out loud from 100. Now, here's the secret to mental relaxation. With each number you say, double your mental relaxation. With each number you say, let your mind become twice as relaxed. Now, if you do this by the time you reach the number 98, or maybe even sooner, your mind will have become so relaxed, you will have actually relaxed all the rest of the numbers that would have come after 98, right out of your mind. And there just won't be any more numbers. Now, you have to do this; I can't do it for you. Those numbers will leave if you will them away. Now start with the idea that you will make that happen and you can easily dispel them from your mind. Want it to happen. Will it to happen. Make it happen. Now, say the first number, 100, and double your mental relaxation. (Client: "100") **Deeper relaxed.** (Wait for client to say number.) **Now, double that mental relaxation and let those numbers already start to fade... 99.** (Client: "99") **Deeper relaxed.** (Wait for client to say number.) **Double your mental relaxation. Start to make those numbers leave. They'll go if you will them away.** (Client: "98") **Deeper relaxed. Now they'll be gone. Dispel them. Banish them. Make it happen, you can do it, I can't do it for you. Put them out. ARE THEY ALL GONE?**

(Usually, the numbers disappear by 98; I've never had a client go past 96. It is your choice whether to prompt the client by saying the number.)

Insert suggestions.

Bring client out of trance.

The number block achieved in Step 6 is a sign that the client is in the same state you get into just before falling asleep. This is Elman's fourth trance level: somnambulism. If you question the client as they are going through the numbers, 100... 99... 98, they will tell you there is a moment when their mind is completely blank. According to Elman, this is when you know that the client has reached full mental relaxation. From a Zen point of view, this is the 'no mind' state, or the void. Leading the client to this state is Elman's objective in doing the numbers. To know that your client has reached this state, you must ask, "Are they [the numbers] all gone?"

An Ericksonian induction is subtle, gentle, and effective. The Progressive Test Induction leads to a particularly deep level of trance. The Elman Induction will result in a trance that is reasonably deep and reasonably quick, and is particularly good as a second induction for a client you have already hypnotized before. It is also a great deal of fun! In order to meet the diverse needs of your clients, it is useful for you to have several different ways of inducing trance.

Elman Induction No. 2

In a moment, you will be examining a second version of the Elman Induction, which follows the same steps as the first but moves more quickly. This second induction works well with a client who has gone through the first induction previously, or has done some trance work before. You might even switch to this second induction if you notice part way through the first induction that you do not seem to be moving fast enough for the client.

After you and your partner have become comfortable with the first Elman induction, practise this second induction together and notice the change of rhythm as the client becomes more used to going into trance. In case the client is moving more slowly than the script, add some of the words from the first Elman induction back in.

Elman Induction No. 2

Take a long, deep breath and close your eyes.

> (Start with your hand above the client's eyes and bring it down to below the chin.)

Now relax the muscles around your eyes to the point where they won't work... and pretend you can't open them even though you know full well that you can. As long as you hold on to this relaxation, you can pretend they just won't work. When you're sure they're so relaxed that they just won't work, continue to pretend

---

that they won't work and test them to make sure THEY WON'T WORK. Test them hard... that's right.

Now let the feeling of relaxation go right down to your toes.

(Assist, using two fingers.)

Now open your eyes—really relax—close your eyes again... that's it... The next time you do this, you'll be able to relax even more than you relaxed before.

Open your eyes... now close your eyes... double the relaxation. Open your eyes... now close your eyes... double the relaxation.

Now I'm going to lift your hand and drop it. I want it to be as limp as a dishrag. Now the moment your hand plops down on your leg, it will send an even deeper relaxation through your whole body. That's right.

We want your mind to be as relaxed as your body is, so I want you to start counting from 100 backwards when I tell you to. Each time you say a number, double your mental relaxation. With each number you say, let your mind become twice as relaxed. By the time you get down to 98, you'll be so relaxed the numbers won't be there. Start from 100 and watch them disappear before you get to 98... double your mental relaxation and watch them start fading... Now watch them disappear.... Now they'll be gone.... Isn't that a nice feeling? Are they all gone? Let them disappear.... Are they all gone? That's right....

Insert suggestions.

Bring client out of trance.

After you have taken turns with your partner doing Elman Induction No. 2, compare notes on which version of Elman each of you preferred as Hypnotherapist and as client. Preferences differ. In the beginning, many Hypnotherapists feel more confident with No. 1 because it allows careful preparation of each step and gives the Hypnotherapist more time to gather their thoughts and proceed smoothly. On the other hand, a client who is used to a fast pace or can go into a trance quickly may become distracted by their own impatience with Induction No. 1. I was once moving at a normal adult speed with an 8-year-old client, who peeked over at me and said, "Would you *hurry up!*"

Chapter 17

Developing Your Induction Style

I again recommend that you practice the Elman Pre-talk and Inductions with a partner until you are doing them smoothly with very little need for the scripts. As you continue to practise, this chapter will offer refinements that can bring you better and better results.

To begin with, be sure you have a comfortable chair for the client, one that is more substantial than an ordinary straight-back chair. If the client feels that they might fall off the chair while in trance, this fear could keep them from readily going into trance. When you're doing hypnotherapy on a regular basis, you may want to invest in a special chair… sometimes clients do very well in a recliner.

At the beginning of your conversation with the client and during the Pre-talk, begin building rapport by matching their posture and movements. If the client is sitting with their legs crossed, cross yours too. If they are leaning to one side a bit, lean at about the same angle. Without knowing why, the client is almost certain to feel comfortable and in rapport with you.

You may remember reaching a special level of rapport in the second Ericksonian induction (Chapter 10) as the result of matching the client's breathing. This attention to breathing can magically increase rapport in an induction. Speak while the client is breathing out. When they breathe in, stop speaking and breathe in with them. You can quickly learn to speak smoothly while matching the client's breathing. It does not matter if this makes you pause in mid-sentence. Matching the client's breathing will not slow down the induction; actually, it will lead you into a rhythm that intensifies rapport and deepens the client's trance.

Here are hints for more easily matching your client's breathing. If you sit straight across from the client looking directly at them, or if they are wearing a jacket or heavy clothes, it may be difficult (or rude!) to observe their breathing. Instead, sit at about a 90-degree angle, and rather than looking at the client, focus your eyes on an object or a spot on the wall that will cause you to be looking a foot or two in front of them. You will actually be able to see the movement of their chest more clearly with your peripheral vision than you could by looking directly at them. This is because our peripheral vision is designed to pick up motion. Sitting at an angle, you will also have the advantage that you can hold your script—if you are using one—at about the level of the client's shoulder, and can easily alternate between glancing at your script and watching the client's breathing in your peripheral vision, without needing to bob your head up and down.

You can also observe breathing by listening. Most obviously, when the client is talking, they are breathing out. More subtly, as you pay close attention, you can often hear light sounds of breathing.

If you notice that the client does not respond as well to matched breathing as they did to an earlier induction without it, by all means omit this normally effective technique.

In addition to noticing the client's breathing, notice everything you can about their physiology and utilize what you see as you are making suggestions. If you notice, for example, that the client is not fully relaxing their neck muscles, you could say, "You may feel that your neck muscles are not totally relaxing yet. And you can just let those relax too."

As you begin an induction, speak to the client with your head upright, talking at a level with the client's face. As the client becomes more and more relaxed and their head begins to nod downwards, allow your own head to gradually move downwards as well. By the time you get to the disappearing numbers step of the Elman Induction, you will be talking to the client's feet.

When you act as the client, you will find that this change in the direction of the Hypnotherapist's voice gives a distinct sensory shift. Your Unconscious Mind will follow the change of direction, and your own physiology will adjust to match the Hypnotherapist's physiology, allowing you to absorb and respond to their suggestions more powerfully.

Pay close attention to the stages of hypnosis. What you will notice is that over repeated inductions, each client's physiology is predictable and will show you what stage has been reached. Generally, the eyelids begin to flutter early in light trance. After some time you'll notice increased wetness in the eyes. Then you'll observe the face becoming more symmetrical. And you'll notice the breathing slowing down dramatically. Finally, you will begin to notice some shifting in the angle of the head. Noticing the client's physiology provides feedback that will allow you to expertly pace the induction.

You can bring the client out of trance early in the session and ask them for feedback. First do a full induction, with some good post-hypnotic suggestions, including one that will make it very easy for them to get back into deep trance again. Then bring the client out. If you ask, "So how did that go?" they are likely to tell you whether the speed of the induction was right for them, and what things you did that helped the process... or didn't. This will be essential feedback if you are not sure what you observed, or if you are still developing your observation skills. Then you can continue the session, leading the client back into trance and adjusting your style according to their feedback.

Be open to experimenting. As you allow your Unconscious Mind to spontaneously supply ideas, especially in utilizing the client's responses, you will often be delighted with the effect on the client. I have said to clients, "As soon as your mind is totally blank, raise your finger to let me know," and they have been able to show me in this way when to go on to the next step.

As the Hypnotherapist, you can allow yourself to go into a waking trance. Erickson frequently said, "It's really hard to resist someone in trance who's hypnotizing you."

Chapter 18

Conclusion

In developing your overall approach as a Hypnotherapist, you will need to build your repertory of inductions through study and practice, and to decide on the full range of interventions that you want to master. I have found it most useful to combine hypnosis, Time-Line Therapy®, and Neuro-Linguistic Programming. This combination provides three complementary avenues to the Unconscious Mind.

Time-Line Therapy® works well in assisting the client to overcome limitations rooted in their early life, or in doing any kind of regression work. Hypnosis is excellent for deep interventions, such as pain control or getting the body to change its responses. NLP is useful for changing behaviours more at a surface level. So, for example, if a client has been referred to you by a medical doctor because they have not responded to the doctor's treatment of their ulcers, you could first use Time-Line Therapy® to go back and get rid of the mental source of the ulcers. Then, using hypnosis, you could talk to the client's Unconscious Mind to get it to heal the body. And if the client loves a food that seems to trigger ulcer attacks, you could use an NLP technique to make that food choice very unattractive. I often use all three methodologies in one session.

You do not usually need a formal induction with Time-Line Therapy®. The process of working with the Time-Line itself is sufficient for inducing a light trance and releasing the mental causes of most of the client's problems that you will be working with. Once you have a Time-Line Therapy® intervention in progress, a deeper hypnotic induction is usually fast and easy.

When Not to Use Hypnosis

To offer the safest and most useful hypnotherapy for your clients, you need to understand the *scope of practice* suitable for a Hypnotherapist who is not licensed. Unless you are a licensed psychologist, medical doctor, dentist, social worker, or marriage, family and child counsellor, you should limit the scope of your practice to stress reduction, performance enhancement, and habit control issues such as smoking and weight loss. If you have a written referral from a medical doctor or you are working in cooperation with a psychiatrist or psychologist, it is appropriate to do additional kinds of work. This is especially important in the United States, where we face fairly heavy restrictions on what Hypnotherapists can do.

There are five instances in which hypnosis is specifically contra-indicated:

• First, when the client's personal history suggests that they may be dangerous to themselves or others, the client is beyond the scope of treatment of an unlicensed Hypnotherapist. In most states of the US, even a psychologist, MFCC or MSW will refer a client who is dangerous to self or others to a psychiatrist or a medical doctor.

• Second, if the client is dealing with highly repressed or traumatic issues, you may want to refer them to someone who has been trained to deal with those issues. Hypnosis alone may not be a sufficient intervention. Time-Line Therapy® could be indicated; if you are not trained in it, you can refer the client to a certified practitioner of Time-Line Therapy®. In addition, it may be appropriate to have a psychiatrist or a psychologist work with the client.

• Third, if a client is dealing with cancer or another life-threatening disease, you should advise them that hypnosis is a controversial form of treatment and insist that they get a diagnosis and a written referral from a medical doctor before proceeding. Currently in the US, it is not illegal to use hypnosis to help alleviate the symptoms of a disease. It is illegal to claim to cure disease by means of hypnosis. In most parts of the world, it is inappropriate to say that you will use hypnosis to cure cancer. Here is what I say to the client: "What is important here is that I am not going to heal you, you are going to heal yourself. Whether or not that happens is going to depend on how well you can communicate with your Unconscious Mind." That is a very important framework for your intervention. You will never regret referring someone out if you have any question on whether you should be working with them.

- Fourth, if a client is suffering from psychiatric or neurological disorders such as multiple personality, schizophrenia, bipolar disorders (manic-depressive), hysteria or epileptic seizures, it is appropriate for you to require a written referral from an MD or psychiatrist before you even consider working with the client.

- Fifth, **you should only hypnotize a member of the opposite sex when there is a reliable witness present.** Erickson, for example, would not hypnotize women unless his wife was present. An alternate safeguard is to tape all your sessions.

Continuous Learning

There is a wealth of resources available as you continue to build your skills in hypnotherapy.

You can pursue an independent study programme offered by the American Pacific University, to earn a Bachelor's degree or a doctorate in Clinical Hypnotherapy. The Institute also offers 'hands-on' training at its main campus in Honolulu, Hawaii and at other locations throughout the US. The phone number for the Institute is 800–800-6463.

A local study group can give you access to the experience and support of colleagues, as well as the chance to further practise what you have learned. To find or form a study group, you can call the Institute for a list of people in your area.

I offer beginning and advanced courses in Neuro-Linguistic Programming and Time-Line Therapy® in North America, Europe, Asia and Australia. The courses emphasize the ties between NLP, Time-Line Therapy® and hypnosis. Information is available from Advanced Neuro Dynamics at 800–800-MIND (6463).

As you build your knowledge and skill in hypnosis and acquaint yourself with NLP, visit our Internet site at:

http://www.hypnosis. com

It gives a complete collection of scripts for hypnosis and NLP, as well as a wealth of further information.

Your most valuable resource for developing your skills is your own Unconscious Mind. I encourage you to talk to it. Listen to it. Trust it.

Appendix

Short Induction Scripts,
Without Directions

Ericksonian Induction No. 1: Question Set Induction

1. Have you ever been in a trance before... right now?
   (*If no:*) Can you remember the state you were in just before you completely woke up this morning?

2. Did you experience that state as being similar to the waking state, or different from the waking state?

3. Can you find a spot that you would like to look at comfortably?

4. As you continue comfortably looking at that spot for a while, do your eyelids want to blink? (That's right.)

5. Will those lids begin to blink one at a time... twice or three times before they close altogether? (That's right.)

6. Rapidly or more slowly? (That's right.)

7. Will they just close, now, or will they flutter all by themselves first?

8. Will the eyes close more and more as you get more and more relaxed?

9. That's right. Can those eyes now remain closed as your comfort...able to go deeper, just like when you go to sleep?

10. Can your comfort go more and more deeply, inside, so that you'd rather not even try to open your eyes?

11. Or would you rather really try in vain and find you cannot?
    And just when will you soon forget about them altogether because your unconscious... wants to dream?
    (Insert suggestions.)
    In a moment, I am going to count backwards from 10 to 1, and I want you to awaken one tenth of the way with each number until you are fully awake. 10... 9... 8... etc.

Ericksonian Induction No.2: Arm Levitation

1. Have you ever been in a trance before… right now?

2. Did you experience that state as being similar to the waking state, or different from the waking state?

3. You can feel comfortable resting your hands gently on your thighs, can you not? That's right, don't let them touch each other.

4. Can those hands rest soo-oo lightly so that the fingertips *just* touch your thighs?

5. That's right. As they rest there just so lightly, have you noticed yet how they tend to lift up a bit all by themselves *with each breath you take? Good. Now we will just wait and see.*

6. Now, can you find a spot that you would like to look at comfortably?

7. As you continue comfortably looking at that spot for a while, do your eyelids want to blink?

8. Will those lids begin to blink one at a time… twice or three times before they close altogether?

9. Rapidly or more slowly?

10. Will they just close, now, or will they flutter all by themselves first?

11. Will the eyes close more and more as you get more and more relaxed?

12. That's right. Can those eyes just stay closed as your comfort… able to go deeper, just like when you go to sleep?

13. Can your comfort go more and more deeply, inside, so that you'd rather not even try to open your eyes?

14.   Or would you rather really try and find you cannot?

15.   And just when will you soon forget about them altogether because your unconscious… wants you to dream!… of lifting, lifting, lifting?

16.   Have you noticed your hands lifting, lifting, lifting, even more easily, and by themselves… as the rest of your body relaxes more and more?

17.   As that goes on, does one hand or the other… or maybe both… continue lifting, lifting, lifting even more?

18.   And does that hand stay up and continue lifting, lifting, lifting even higher and higher all by itself? Does the other hand want to catch up with it and go up too, or will the other hand just relax in your lap?

19.   That's right. And does the hand continue lifting, lifting, lifting as it is, or will the lifting get smoother or less smooth as the hand continues upward toward your face?
Now… Does the hand slow down or go faster and faster as it approaches your face deepening your comfort? Will it… pause a bit before it finally touches your face so you'll know you are really going into a trance? And it won't touch until your Unconscious… is really, really ready to let you go deeper… will it?
And… will your body automatically take a deeper breath when that hand… touches your face and you really relax and experience yourself going deeper and deeper?

That's right. And will you even bother to notice you're deepening the comfortable as that hand slowly goes back to your lap all by itself? And will your Unconscious be in a dream by the time that hand comes to rest?

(Insert suggestions.)

In a moment, I am going to count backwards from 10 to 1, and I want you to awaken one tenth of the way with each number until you are fully awake. 10 … 9 … 8 … etc."

General Hypnosis Paradigm

A.   **PREPARATION**. Define desired outcome. Obtain personal history. Accomplish pre-talk and suggestibility tests.

B.   **INDUCTION**. Use a formal or informal trance induction.

C.   **UTILIZATION**. Utilize all of client's behaviour to help them achieve and deepen trance. Utilize hypnotic phenomena to gauge client's level of trance.

CHANGE WORK

• Does your Unconscious Mind know what to do to solve the problem?

• Is it possible for your Unconscious Mind to heal the condition?

• Is it all right to heal this now or to organize the steps now for healing?

• Are there any other problems your Unconscious Mind would like to work on?

• Unconscious Mind, go ahead and heal (client's name).

• How quickly will your Unconscious Mind start the healing? How quickly will it finish?

BRINGING THE CLIENT OUT

Progressive Test Induction Adapted From Estabrooks

Close Eyes – Talk Sleep

Now, if you would like to just go ahead and see if you can close your eyes. And I wonder if you can imagine, everybody can, imagining is something you can do, remember how much you imagined when you were little, or you can just remember a time when you were falling asleep (*yawn*), just falling sound asleep. Now, perhaps you can remember a time when you were soo-oo tired, and relaxed... all your muscles totally... relax... and just remember a time when you were falling asleep, going into a deep sleep. Deeper and deeper and deeper (etc). That's right. Now, this is important, you can stay asleep as long as you want to stay asleep until I tell you, and remember, you will always hear the sound of my voice, however far or deep you go and you will always feel just fine and be just fine as a result of these suggestions. So, it's OK, just go ahead and fall sound, sound asleep. Deeper and deeper and deeper asleep. (*Continue for 5 minutes.*) You may or may not remember to forget everything that happens. It's OK.

Eyelids Locked Closed

Now, listen. As deeply relaxed as you are, you still know your eyes are closed, and you may not have noticed that your eyelids feel so heavy that they are, and they really ARE locked so tightly together that you may find it quite amusing to discover that your eyes are locked tight, tight, tightly together. That's right. Your eyelids are locked tightly together and you cannot open your eyes no matter how hard you try, and REALLY try, the tighter they become. And you might care to try, so go ahead, I dare you to try and find with some amusement that you cannot.

Relaxation. Now relax everything. Relax your eyelids. They are returning to normal, and you are sound asleep. Sound, sound asleep, and you will sleep until I tell you.

Then you will awaken quietly and easily... until then, just relax everything and sleep, sleep, sleep.

Stiff Arm

Now it's time for our next test. So just notice your right arm, right where it is (*describe*) is becoming stiff and rigid, rigid and stiff. Stiff and rigid. And everyone knows how a piece of iron feels, so rigid and stiff, just like you ... cannot bend your right arm. It's as if it was an iron bar, solid, rigid, and stiff. It is impossible to bend your right arm's so stiff. I dare you to find with some amusement you cannot. That's right.

Relaxation. Now relax everything. Relax your right arm. It is returning to normal, and you are sound asleep. Sound, sound asleep, and you will sleep until I tell you. Then you will awaken quietly and easily... until then, just relax everything and sleep, sleep, sleep.

Weak Legs

Now, even though you never thought of this before, now notice it's as if your body is floating away, floating away, floating away. And you may discover with some delight that you cannot control the muscles in your legs, you are so relaxed now. And where were you born? Do you remember? Remember! Being a little newborn baby... And now, like then, you're stuck where you are, and your legs won't work, too relaxed. That's right. It is impossible for you to even try to stand up, too relaxed. And the harder you may try, the more relaxed your legs. You are just stuck there in the chair. You may try, and really try, I dare you.

Relaxation. Now relax everything. Relax your legs. They are returning to normal, and you are sound asleep. Sound, sound asleep, and you will sleep until I tell you. Then you will awaken quietly and easily... until then, just relax everything and sleep, sleep, sleep.

Automatic Movement

Now listen carefully, more fun. It's time for us to discover just what your hands can do. In a moment, I'm going to touch your hands. Now, let's start your hands rotating. Here they go. Here they go, round and around. Faster and faster. Can your Unconscious… keep them moving? That's right. They ARE rotating faster and faster. And you just might find with some delight you cannot stop them. You cannot stop, no matter how hard you try, the harder you try, the faster they go around and around.

Relaxation. Now relax everything. Relax your hands. They are returning to rest on your lap, and you are sound asleep. Sound, sound asleep, and you will sleep until I tell you. Then you will awaken quietly and easily… until then, just relax everything and sleep, sleep, sleep.

Talking in Your Sleep

Now I want you to dream, and REALLY dream of talking in your sleep. Everyone knows of someone who talks in their sleep. So sleep and have that dream. Now I am going to ask you a few simple questions, and you can just remain asleep in your dream, and dream you answer me in your sleep, talking in your sleep as you have seen people talk in their sleep. Soon I'm going to ask questions you will find it easy to answer… here they are:

- What is your name?
- What is your address?

Relaxation. Now relax everything. Your voice is again silent and you are sound asleep. Sound, sound asleep, and you will sleep until I tell you. Then you will awaken quietly and easily… until then, just relax everything and sleep, sleep, sleep.

Sleep Walking

Now in a moment you will stand up. I will help you. You will remain asleep as you stand up, as if you were in a dream. You have seen sleepwalkers. Finding it easy to stand up. Now I'm going to touch you, to help you. Go ahead, stand up. Walk. That's right. You are finding it easy to use your leg muscles as you remain deeply asleep. Standing up. And as you sit down, go even more deeply asleep. You can sit down safely and comfortably.

Relaxation. Now relax everything. Relax your legs. They are returning to normal, and you are sound asleep. Sound, sound asleep, and you will sleep until I tell you. Then you will awaken quietly and easily... until then, just relax everything and sleep, sleep, sleep.

Visual Hallucinations

Now listen carefully. In a moment you're going to awaken from the neck up only. Your mind can remain asleep, and your body can remain asleep, but just your head with no recognition of your body can awaken from the neck up. When you're ready, just open your eyes. Open them now, and remain deeply asleep. You are still dreaming and I want you to dream of this tennis ball. Open your eyes and look at the tennis ball in my hand. What color is it? Now I'm going to turn the ball a little bit so you can see the number on it. Once you've got the color and the number, you can close your eyes, staying deeply, deeply asleep.

Relaxation. Now relax everything. Your eyes are returning to normal, and you are sound asleep. Sound, sound asleep, and you will sleep until I tell you. Then you will awaken quietly and easily... until then, just relax everything and sleep, sleep, sleep.

Insert Post-Hypnotic Suggestions. Now in a moment I am going to give your Unconscious Mind some suggestions, which

I would like your Conscious Mind to forget. Forgetting is normal and natural. Forgetting is a normal, natural thing... you do it all the time. Why would you care what you had for lunch two weeks ago, on Wednesday, when it rained? You simply forget it. I want you to forget consciously what I am about to tell you in just a moment. Somebody gives you a slip of paper and you forget about it. Where did it go? Who knows, who cares, just forget about it. Forgetting is a normal, natural thing. Now, I would like to suggest that... (Make suitable positive, direct suggestions!) And I want you to forget my suggestions consciously and remember them unconsciously... like the piece of paper you've forgotten about... like who cares what you had for lunch two weeks ago. It's OK, forgetting's a normal, natural thing. Forget what I just said.

Clear Test or Short-Term Suggestions

Now with your eyes closed, stay deeply asleep for a little while longer. All suggestions I have given you about this trance and all related tests are now removed. All on-going suggestions are still in effect.

Bring the Client out of Trance

Now when you are ready, begin to come back. In a moment, I am going to count backwards from 10 to 1, and I want you to awaken one tenth of the way with each number until you are fully awake. 10... 9... 8... etc.

Full Body Catalepsy

(Optional addition to "Progressive Test Induction Based on Estabrooks")

You have the option of adding a powerful extra convincer to the Progressive Test Induction, following Visual Hallucinations. This option is Full Body Catalepsy. Before considering this option, determine whether the subject has knee, back or neck problems; if they have, do not attempt this test.

We did not include Full Body Catalepsy in the script for the Progressive Test Induction because it is safest to induce this state only with two people present to help with moving the body to the suspended position. It is especially important to be sure that the shoulders are well supported, to avoid possible injury to the neck. This dramatically convincing option is used more commonly in the training of Hypnotherapists than in providing therapy for clients.

To induce full body catalepsy, tell the subject to have their whole body become stiff and rigid. Once they are experiencing full body catalepsy, lean their body back *so that their shoulders are solidly supported on the seat of a straight chair*. In case the floor is slippery and the subject is wearing leather-soled shoes, an assistant needs to hold the subject's ankles to prevent sliding as you are leaning them back. Now raise the ankles and feet and slide a second chair under them. The subject's cataleptic body will then be suspended in mid-air, completely rigid. (Do *not* put a person or any weight on the subject; this could cause injury.)

To bring the subject back up, remove the chair from under their feet, and lower the feet. Steady the feet against sliding if necessary, and raise the body to standing position. Say, "Remaining in trance, just go ahead and relax." Push a chair gently against the backs of the subject's legs and tell them to sit back down.

If you are not sure as 'subject' whether to experience full body catalepsy, ask your Unconscious Mind what to do. There is no reason to experience this test unless you have the desire. I have had instances of students with minor back problems consulting their Unconscious Minds and deciding to go ahead with full body catalepsy. Some of them have seemed to experience a back improvement from the tightening of the muscles, and they discovered they could do something they didn't think they could do.

Elman Pre-Talk

Make a fist. Relax.

You know that if you wanted to, you could tighten your muscles and make a fist that was so strong that you couldn't make it any stronger or any more powerful. Isn't that true? So, if you wanted, and if you knew how, you could also make any group of muscles you wanted so absolutely, totally relaxed that unless you removed the relaxation, you could relax those muscles to the point where they wouldn't work. That is also true, isn't it?

Eyelids are the easiest to relax.

The easiest group of muscles in your entire body to relax are your eyelids. Now, you know that's true, don't you? Remember a time when you were tired, had a rough day, and you closed your eyes, and it just feels so good.

"Now, watch what I do."

I'm going to close my eyes, and I am going to relax them so completely and so deeply that if I do not take that relaxation away, they won't work. Nothing that I can do or say or think will make them open. Now I can take away the relaxation and they will open instantly, but if the relaxation is there, they won't work.

Now I'm going to try to open my eyes. (*Open eyes.*) Now I tested myself to see that they did work, and I did the wrong thing, because I wanted to test them to be sure they do not work.

"This time I am going to keep them shut."

This time I am going to relax my eyelids to the point where they won't work. And I am going to hold on to the relaxation and then test them to make sure they do *not* work. I don't have to prove they will work, I can do that every day. I know that I can instantly remove the relaxation by the slightest thought, the slightest desire, so I am not going to do that this time. This time I'm going to allow them to stay totally relaxed, and I know that as long as I stay totally relaxed, and as long as I do not take that relaxation away, nothing I can do or say or think will cause them to open. Watch. See, they stay there like an old shoe. And I know it looks stupid with my eyebrows going up and down, but it feels great!

"You can do it too!"

Now, I can feel proud of myself, because I did it. I can take the relaxation away and I can open my eyes. You know, 5-year-old kids can do this; you can do this, too. Just see if you can do what I do. Close your eyes, and put your awareness on your eyelids. You're in charge, you're in control, and your muscles have to do what you tell them to do.

"They respond to what you tell them."

Not what I tell them to do… they respond to you, not me. Your eyelids respond to you because the suggestions are coming directly from you, and through your neurology. You direct your body to follow those suggestions totally and completely, and you will be successful.

Have the client do it.

So, go ahead, tell your body to relax your eyelid muscles totally and completely, so deeply and completely that unless you remove the relaxation, they just won't work. And when you know that you have accomplished this, then hold on to the relaxation and give them a good test, and notice that they stay shut; make sure they won't work, and notice how good that feels. Test them hard, really try.

(*If* client opens eyes:) Congratulations; now prove you can relax them so they won't work.

Conclusion

That was the hardest step. You did just great.

Elman Induction No.1

Take a long, deep breath and hold it for a few seconds. And as you exhale this breath, allow your eyes to close (*Pass fingers*), and let go of the surface tension in your body. Just let your body relax as much as possible, right now.

Now place your awareness on your eye muscles, and relax the muscles around your eyes to the point where they just won't work. When you're sure they're so relaxed that as long as you hold on to this relaxation they won't work, hold on to that relaxation and test them to make sure THEY WON'T WORK.

Now, this relaxation you have in your eyes is the same quality of relaxation that I want you to have throughout your whole body. So let this quality of relaxation flow through your whole body from the top of your head to the tips of your toes.

Now we can deepen this relaxation much more. In a moment I'm going to have you open and close your eyes. When you close your eyes, that's your signal to let this feeling of relaxation become ten times deeper. All you have to do is want it to happen, and you can make it happen very easily. OK, now, open your eyes. Now close your eyes (*Pass fingers*) and feel that relaxation flowing through your entire body, taking you much deeper. Use your wonderful imagination and imagine your whole body is covered and wrapped in a warm blanket of relaxation. Now we can deepen that relaxation much more. In a moment, I'm going to have you open and close your eyes and double the relaxation you have now. Make it become twice as deep. Once more now, open your eyes. Close your eyes (*Pass fingers*) and double your relaxation... good. Let every muscle in your body become so relaxed that as long as you hold on to this quality of relaxation, every muscle of your body is totally relaxed.

In a moment, I'm going to have you open and close your eyes once more. Again, when you close your eyes, double the relaxation you now have. Make it twice as deep. Once more, open your eyes... close your eyes and double your relaxation... good. Let every muscle in your body become so relaxed that as long as you hold on to this quality of relaxation, every muscle of your body is totally relaxed.

In a moment I'm going to lift your hand by the wrist just a few inches, and drop it. If you have followed my instructions up to this point, that hand will be so relaxed it will be just as loose and limp as a wet dish cloth. It will simply plop down. Now, don't try to help me...you have to remove the realization and let me do all the lifting, so that when I release your hand, it just plops down and you'll allow yourself to go much deeper. Now the moment your hand plops down on your leg, it will send an even deeper relaxation through your whole body. Now, that's complete physical relaxation. I want you to know there are two ways a person can relax. You can relax physically and you can relax mentally. You've already proved that you can relax physically. Now let me show you how to relax mentally.

In a moment, I'll ask you to begin slowly counting backwards out loud from 100. Now, here's the secret to mental relaxation. With each number you say, double your mental relaxation. With each number you say, let your mind become twice as relaxed. Now, if you do this, by the time you reach the number 98, or maybe even sooner, your mind will have become so relaxed, you will have actually relaxed all the rest of the numbers that would have come after 98, right out of your mind. And there just won't be any more numbers. Now, you have to do this; I can't do it for you. Those numbers will leave if you will them away. Now start with the idea that you will make that happen and you can easily dispel them from your mind. Want it to happen. Will it to happen. Make it happen.

Now, say the first number, 100, and double your mental relaxation. Deeper relaxed.

Now, double that mental relaxation and let those numbers already start to fade... 99. Deeper relaxed.

Double your mental relaxation. Start to make those numbers leave. They'll go if you will them away. Deeper relaxed. Now they'll be gone. Dispel them. Banish them. Make it happen, you can do it, I can't do it for you. Put them out. ARE THEY ALL GONE?

Insert suggestions.

Bring client out of trance.

Elman Induction No.2

Take a long, deep breath and close your eyes.

Now relax the muscles around your eyes to the point where they won't work... and pretend you can't open them even though you know full well that you can. As long as you hold on to this relaxation, you can pretend they just won't work. When you're sure they're so relaxed that they just won't work, continue to pretend that they won't work and test them to make sure THEY WON'T WORK. Test them hard... that's right.

Now let the feeling of relaxation go right down to your toes.

Now open your eyes—really relax—close your eyes again... that's it... The next time you do this, you'll be able to relax even more than you have relaxed.

Open your eyes... now close your eyes... double the relaxation.

Open your eyes... now close your eyes... double the relaxation.

Now I'm going to lift your hand and drop it. I want it to be as limp as a dishrag. Now the moment your hand plops down on your leg, it will send an even deeper relaxation through your whole body. That's right.

We want your mind to be as relaxed as your body is, so I want you to start counting from 100 backwards when I tell you to. Each time you say a number, double your mental relaxation. With each number you say, let your mind become twice as relaxed. By the time you get down to 98, you'll be so relaxed the numbers won't be there. Start from 100 and watch them disappear before you get to 98... double your mental relaxation and watch them start fading.... Now watch them disappear... Now they'll be gone... Isn't that a nice feeling? Are they all gone? Let them disappear…. Are they all gone? That's right….

Insert suggestions.

Bring client out of trance.

Bibliography

Adams, Paul (1967, 1978). *The New Self Hypnosis*, Los Angeles, Wilshire Book Company.

Alman, Brian & Peter Lambrou (1983, 1992). *Self Hypnosis*, New York, Brunner Mazel.

Arons, Harry (1967). *Handbook of Self-Hypnosis*, Irvington, NJ, Power Publishers.

Arons, Harry (1969, 1978). *Prize Winning Methods of Hypnosis*, Irvington, NJ, Power Publishers.

Arons, Harry (1953). *Techniques of Speed Hypnosis*, S. Orange, NJ, Theo Gaus.

Arons, Harry (1948, 1955, 1961). *The New Master Course in Hypnosis*, Irvington, NJ, Power Publishers.

Atkinson, William Walker (1912, 1940). *Memory Culture*, Chicago, IL, Psychic Research Co. (Yogi Pub Society) (Reprinted by Kessinger Publishing Co., Kila, MT, 1998).

Atkinson, William Walker (1907). *Mental Fascination*, London, L.N.Fowler (Reprinted by Kessinger Publishing Co., Kila, MT, 1996).

Atkinson, William Walker (1912, 1940, 1997). *Mind Power: The Secret of Mental Magnetism*, Chicago, IL, Yogi Publication Society.

Atkinson, William Walker (1910). *Practical Mental Influence & Mental Fascination*, Chicago, IL, Yogi Publication Society (Reprinted by Kessinger Publishing Co., Kila, MT, 1998).

Atkinson, William Walker (1901). *Thought Force in Business and Everyday Life*, Chicago, IL, The Psychic Research Company.

Atkinson, William Walker (1910). *Practical Mind Reading*, Chicago, IL, Yogi Publication Society.

Atkinson, William Walker (1910). *Reincarnation & The Law of Karma*, Chicago, IL, Yogi Publication Society (Reprinted by Kessinger Publishing Co., Kila, MT, 1996).

Atkinson, William Walker (1915). *Subconscious & Superconscious Planes of Mind*, London, L.N. Fowler (Reprinted by Kessinger Publishing Co., Kila, MT, 1998).

Atkinson, William Walker (1909). *Suggestion and Auto Suggestion*, Chicago, IL, The Progress Company (Reprinted by Kessinger Publishing Co., Kila, MT, 1997).

Atkinson, William Walker (1915). *Suggestion & Auto-Suggestion*, London, L.N. Fowler (Reprinted by Kessinger Publishing Co., Kila, MT, 1996).

Atkinson, William Walker (1915). *The Art of Expression*, London, L.N. Fowler.

Atkinson, William Walker (1915). *The Art of Logical Thinking*, London, L.N. Fowler.

Atkinson, William Walker (1912). *The New Psychology*, Holyoke, MA, The Elizabeth Townd Co. (Reprinted by Health Research, 1996).

Atkinson, William Walker (1915). *The New Psychology: Its Message*, Principles & Practice London, L.N. Fowler (Reprinted by Kessinger Publishing Co., Kila, MT, 1996).

Atkinson, William Walker (1915). *The Psychology of Success*, London, L.N. Fowler.

Atkinson, William Walker (1915). *The Will*, London, L.N. Fowler.

Atkinson, William Walker (1915). *Thought Culture or Practical Mental Training*, London, L.N. Fowler.

Barth, George (1851). *The Mesmerist's Manual of Phenomena and Practice*, London, H. Bailliere (Reprinted by Health Research, 1998).

Baudouin, Charles (1920). *Suggestion and Auto Suggestion*, New South Wales, George Allen & Unwin.

Berhardt, Jules (1968). *Self Hypnosis, The Miracle of the Mind*, North Hollywood, CA, Institute for Dynamic Living.

Bernheim, H. (1889, 1947). *Suggestive Therapeutics*, London, London Book Company.

Binet, Alfred & Charles Fere (1887). *Animal Magnetism*, London, Kegan, Paul, Trench & Co.

Binet, Alfred (1890). *On Double Consciousness*, Chicago, IL, The Open Court Publishing Co.

Birns, H.D. (1968). *Hypnosis: Unleash Power of Your Mind Without Drugs*, New York, Award Books.

Block, Ed & F.A. Mesmer (1980). *Mesmerism*, Los Angeles, William Kauffman.

Bodie, Walford (1905). *The Bodie Book of Hypnotism, Electricity, Mental Suggestion, Magnetic Touch, Clairvoyance, Telepathy*, London, The Claxton Press.

Braid, James (1843). *Braid on Hypnotism* (Neurypnology), New York, Julian Press.

Braid, James (1846). *The Power of the Mind Over the Body*, London, John Churchill.

Bramwell, J. Milne (1903). *Hypnotism—Its History Practice & Theory*, London, Grant Richards.

Brenman, Margaret & Merton Gill (1947). *Hypnotherapy: Survey of the Literature*, New York, John Wiley & Sons.

Brooks, C. Harry (1922). *The Practice of Auto Suggestion*, Dodd, Mead and Company.

Brooks, C. Harry (1922, 1940). *The Practice of Auto Suggestion by the Method of E. Coue*, New South Wales, George Allen & Unwin.

Brown, William (1922). *Suggestion and Mental Analysis*, London, University of London Press.

Bryan, William (1962). *Legal Aspects of Hypnosis*, Springfield, IL, Charles Thomas Publishers.

Buranelli, Vincent (1975). *The Wizard from Vienna*, New York, Coward, McCann & Co.

Cannon, Alexander (1936). *The Science of Hypnotism*, New York, E.P. Dutton (Reprinted by Kessinger Publishing Co., Kila, MT, 1998).

Caprio, Frank & Joseph Be (1963). *Helping Yourself with Self-Hypnosis*, Engelwood Cliffs, NJ, Prentice Hall.

Chaney, Robert G. (1958). *Occult Hypnotism*, Upland, CA, Astara.

Cocke, James R (1897). *Hypnotism: How It Is Done; Its Uses and Dangers*, Boston, Lee and Shepard Publishers.

Colquhoun, J.C. (1833). *Animal Magnetism; Reports on Experiments*, New York, Arno Press (New York Times Press).

Cook, William Wesley (1901). *Practical Lessons in Hypnotism*, New York, Willey Book Co.

Corbett, Margaret (1953). *How to Improve Your Sight*, New York, Bonanza Books.

Cotes, James (1890). *How to Mesmerize*, Manual of Instruction, Philadelphia, David McKay Company.

Coue, Emile (1923). *My Method*, New York, Doubleday, Page & Co.

Crabtree, Adam (1988). *Animal Magnetism, Early Hypnotism, & Psychical Research 1766-1925*, White Plains, NY, Kraus International Publishers.

Darnton, Robert (1968). *Mesmerism and the End of Enlightenment*, Cambridge, MA, Harvard University Press.

Davis, Albert E. (1918). *Hypnotism and Treatment by Suggestion*, London, Simpkin, Marshall, Hamilton, Kent & Co. Ltd.

De Saint Germain, Comte C. (1901). *Practical Hypnotism, Theories & Experiments: Ancient Mystery Unveiled*, Chicago, IL, Laird & Lee.

De Duboir, Georges (1922). *Mysteries of Hypnosis*, London, William Rider & Son.

De Laurence, L.W. (1902). *Practical Lessons in Hypnotism and Magnetism*, Chicago, IL, The De Laurence Co.

Deleuze, J.P.F. (1816). '*A Critical History of Animal Magnetism*', #1 Issue of the Magnetizer's Magazine, July 1816.

Deleuze, J.P.F. (1843, 1879, 1890). *Report of the Experiments on Animal Magnetism*, New York, Fowler & Welles Co.

Dods, John Bovee (1886). *The Philosophy of Mesmerism, and Electrical Psychology*, London, James Burns.

Dresser, Annetta Gertrude (1895). *The Philosophy of P.P. Quimby*, Los Angeles, Devorss & Co.

Dumont, Theron Q. (1914). *The Advanced Course in Personal Magnetism*, London, L.N. Fowler.

Dumont, Theron Q. (1913). *The Art and Science of Personal Magnetism*, Chicago, IL, Yogi Publication Society (Reprinted by Health Research, 1993).

Dumont, Theron Q. (1913, 1972). *Mental Therapeutics*, Chicago, IL, Yogi Publication Society.

Dumont, Theron Q. (1914). *Personal Magnetism: Advanced Course*, Chicago, IL, Advanced Thought Publishers.

Dumont, Theron Q. (1913, 1930). *Personal Magnetism*, Chicago, IL, Yogi Publication Society.

Dumont, Theron Q. (1913). *Personal Magnetism: The Secrets of Mental Fascination*, London, L.N. Fowler.

Eaves, Osborne (1918). *Your Powers and How to Use Them*, Harrogate, Yorkshire, Talisman Publishers.

Edmunds, Simeon (1961). *Hypnotism and Psychic Phenomena*, Los Angeles, Wilshire Press.

Eldridge, Edward (1901). *Hypnotism: What It Is, How to Do It*, Clevland, OH, The Arthur Westbrook Company.

Elliot, K. (1975, 1981). *Hypnotism Theory and Practice*, Toronto, Coles Publishing Company.

Ellsworth, Robert G. (1902). *The Key to Hypnotism*, Philadelphia, David McKay Publishers.

Elman, Dave (1964). *Hypnotherapy*, Glenndale, CA, Westwood Publishing.

Erickson, Milton (1992). *Creative Choice In Hypnosis*, New York, Irvington Publishers.

Erickson, Milton (Sidney Rosen ed.) (1982). *My Voice Will Go With You*, New York, W.W. Norton.

Erickson, Milton & Cooper (1982). *Time Distortion in Hypnosis*, New York, Irvington Publishers.

Erickson, Milton & David Gordon (1981). *Phoenix*, Cupertino, CA, Meta Publications.

Erickson, Milton, Seymour Hershman & Irving I. Secter (1961). *The Practical Application of Medical and Dental Hypnosis*, New York, Julian Press.

Erickson, Milton & E. Rossi (1981). *Experiencing Hypnosis*, New York, Irvington Publishers.

Erickson, Milton & E. Rossi (1983). *Healing In Hypnosis*, New York, Irvington Publishers.

Erickson, Milton & E. Rossi (1979). *Hypnotherapy*, New York, Irvington Publishers.

Erickson, Milton & E. Rossi (1976). *Hypnotic Realities*, New York, Irvington Publishers.

Erickson, Milton & E. Rossi (1985). *Life Reframing in Hypnosis*, New York, Irvington Publishers.

Erickson, Milton & E. Rossi (1986). *Mind Body Communication in Hypnosis*, New York, Irvington Publishers.

Erickson, Milton & E. Rossi (1989). *The February Man*, New York, Brunner Mazel.

Esdaile, James (1850, 1960). *Mesmerism in India (Hypnosis in Medicine & Surgery)*, New York, Julian Press/Institute for Research in Hypnosis.

Estabrooks, George (1962). *Hypnosis: Current Problems*, New York, Harper & Row.

Estabrooks, George H. (1943). *Hypnotism*, New York, E.P. Dutton.

Estabrooks, George H.(1947). *Spiritism*, New York, E.P. Dutton.

Estabrooks, George H. & N. Gross (1961). *The Future of the Human Mind*, London, The Museum Press Ltd.

Forel, August (1927). *Psychotherapy and Suggestion or Hypnotism*, New York, Allied Publishing Co.

Franquin (1954). *Open Your Mind-Course/Mind Control*, Sydney, Robyn Publications.

Freytag, Fredricka F. (1959). *The Hypnoanalysis of an Anxiety System*, New York, The Julian Press.

Fromm, Erika & Ronald Shor (1972). *Hypnosis: Research Development*, Chicago, IL, Aldine Publishers.

Fross, Garland (1979). *The Handbook of Hypnotic Techniques*, South Orange, NJ, Power Publishers.

Fry, T.C. (1989). *The Great Aids Hoax*, Manchaca, Health Excellence Systems.

Fuller, Robert C. (1982). *Mesmerism and American Cure of Souls*, Philadelphia, PA, University of Pensylvania Press.

Furst, Arnold (1969). *Post Hypnotic Instructions*, Los Angeles, Wilshire Publishing Co.

Furst, Arnold (1982). *Rapid Induction Hypnosis and Suggestion*, Los Angeles, Borden Publishing Co.

Germain, Walter (1981). *Hypnotism, Theory & Practice*, Toronto, Coles Publishing Company Ltd.

Germain, Walter (1956). *The Magic Power of Your Mind*, New York, Hawthorn Books.

Gibson, Walter (1961). *Hypnotism Through the Ages*, New York, Vista House Publishing.

Gibson, Walter (1956). *The Key to Hypnotism*, New York, Key Book Co.

Gilligan, Stephen (1987). *Therapeutic Trances*, New York, Brunner Mazel.

Gindes, Bernard (1951). *New Concepts of Hypnosis*, Los Angeles, Wilshire Press.

Goulding, Mary & Robert Goulding (1979). *Changing Lives Through Redecision Therapy*, New York, Brunner Mazel.

Hadley, Josie and Carol Staudac (1985). *Hypnosis for Change*, Oakland, New Harbinger Publishers.

Haley, Jay (1967). *Advanced Techniques of Hypnosis of MH Erickson*, New York, Grune & Stratton Publishers.

Haley, Jay (1985). *Conversations With Milton H. Erickson*, New York, Triangle Press.

Haley, Jay (1986). *The Power Tactics of Jesus Christ*, New York, Triangle Press.

Hall, Manly Palmer (1939, 1948). *Hypnotism*, Los Angeles, CA, Philosophical Research Society.

Hamblin, Henry Thomas (1921). *Dynamic Thought*, Chicago, IL, Yogi Publication Society.

Harris, Errol E. (1965). *The Foundations of Metaphysics in Science*, New York, Humanities Press.

Hart, Ernest (1896). *Hypnotism, Mesmerism and Witchcraft*, Toronto, Coles Reprint.

Haven, Joseph (1857). *Mental Philosophy*, New York, Sheldon & Co.

Havens, Ronald & Catherine Walters (1989). *Hypnotherapy Scripts*, New York, Brunner Mazel.

Heidenhan, Rudolf (1888). *Hypnotism or Animal Magnetism*, London, Kegan, Paul, Trench & Co.

Heron, William T. (1950,1957). *Clinical Applications of Suggestion and Hypnosis*, Springfield, IL, Charles C. Thomas Publishers.

Hewitt, William W. (1987). *Beyond Hypnosis: A Program for Developing Your Psychic and Healing Powers*, St. Paul MN, Llewellyn Publications.

Hilgard, Ernest & Josephine Hilgard (1975, 1983). *Hypnosis in the Relief of Pain*, Los Altos, CA, William Kaufman.

Hilgard, Ernest (1965). *Hypnotic Susceptibility*, Jovanovich, New York, Harcourt Brace.

Hjelle, Larry & Daniel Zeigler (1991). *Personality Theories*, New York, McGraw Hill.

Hock, Conrad (1934). *The Four Temperaments*, Milwaukee, The Bruce Publishing Co.

Hollander, Bernard (1910). *Hypnotism and Suggestion in Daily Life & Medical Practice*, New York, G.P. Putnam's Sons.

Hollander, Bernard (1957). *Methods and Uses of Hypnosis*, Los Angeles, Wilshire Press.

Hubbard, L. Ron (1951, 1975). *Dianetics Today*, Los Angeles, The Church of Scientology.

Hubbard, L. Ron (1951, 1968). *Self Analysis*, Los Angeles, The Church of Scientology.

Hudson, Thomson Jay (1893, 1904). *The Law of Psychic Phenomena*, Chicago, IL, A.C. McClurg & Co. (Reprinted by Book Sales Incorporated, 1995).

Humphrey, George (1923). *The Story of Man's Mind*, Cambridge, Mass., Murray Printing Company.

Husson, Mr. (1836). *Report on the Magnetical Experiments*, Boston, D.K. Hitchcock.

Ince, R.B. (1920). *Franz Anton Mesmer – His Life*, London, Kegan, Paul, Trench & Co.

James, William (1890). *Principles of Psychology* (2 vols), New York, Henry Holt & Co. (Reprinted by Harvard University Press, 1983).

James, William (1909). *Psychology – Briefer Course* (2 vols), New York, Henry Holt & Co. (Reprinted by University of Notre Dame Press, 1985).

James, William (1902, 1961). *Varieties of Religious Experience*, New York, Collier Books (Reprinted by Random House, 1999).

Jolowicz, Ernst & Gustav Heyer (1931). *Suggestion Therapy/ Hypnosis*, London, C.W. Daniel & Co.

Kahn, Samuel (1945). *Suggestion and Hypnotism Made Practical*, Boston, Meador Publishing Co.

Kaplan, Fred (1982). *John Ellitson on Mesmerism*, New York, DaCapo Press.

Kappas, John (1984). *Improve Your Sex Life Through Self-Hypnosis*, Van Nuys, CA, Panorama Publishing Co.

Kappas, John (1975, 1987). *Professional Hypnotism Manual,* Engelwood Cliffs, NJ, Prentice Hall.

Kelly, Sean & Reid Kelly (1985). *Hypnosis: Understanding How It Can Work for You*, Reading, MA, Addison Wesley.

Kingsbury, George (1891, 1959). *The Practice of Hypnotic Suggestion*, Hollywood, CA, Wilshire Press.

Kingsland, William (1924). *Rational Mysticism*, London, George Allen & Unwin, Ltd.

Kline, Milton V. (1958). *Freud and Hypnosis*, New York, Julian Press.

Klippstein, Hildegard (1991). *Ericksonian Hypnotherapeutic Group Inductions*, New York, Brunner Mazel.

Korth, Leslie O. (1958). *Curative Hypnosis*, London, Thorsons.

Krasner, A.M. (1990). *The Wizard Within*, Irvine, CA, ABH Press.

Krebs, Stanley L. (1906). *The Funamental Principles of Hypnosis* (originally *The Law of Suggestion*), New York, Julian Press.

Kuhn, Lesley & Salvatore Russo (1958). *Modern Hypnosis*, Los Angeles, Wilshire Press.

Lankton, Stephen R. ed. (1989). *Ericksonian Hypnosis: Monograph*, New York, Brunner Mazel.

Lankton, Stephen R. & Carol A. Lankton (1983). *The Answer Within*, New York, Brunner Mazel.

Leitner, Konradi (1953). *Hypnotism for Professionals*, New York, Stravon Publishers.

LeCron, Leslie (1964). *Self Hypnotism* (2 vols), Engelwood Cliffs, NJ, Prentice Hall.

LeCron, Leslie ed. (1948,1952). *Experimental Hypnosis*, New York, MacMillan Publishers.

LeCron, Leslie & J. Bordeau (1949). *Hypnotism Today* (2 vols), New York, Grune & Stratton.

LeCron, Leslie et al. (1961) *Techniques of Hypnotherapy*, New York, Julian Press.

LeCron, Leslie (1971). *The Complete Guide to Hypnosis*, New York, Harper & Row.

Lloyd, B. Layton (1934). *Hypnotism in the Treatment of Disease*, London, John Bale, Sons & Danielson, Ltd.

Lovatt, William (1933). *Hypnosis and Suggestion*, Paternoster Row, UK, Rider & Co.

Loveland, J.S. (1889). *Lectures on Mediumship*, Chicago, IL, Moses Hull & Co.

Lovern, John (1991). *Pathways to Reality*, New York, Brunner Mazel.

Magonet, A. Philip (1957). *Hypnosis in Medicine*, Los Angeles, CA, Wilshire Press.

Marcuse, F. L. (1959). *Hypnosis: Fact and Fiction*, Baltimore, MD, Penguin Books.

Marks, Robert W. (1947). *The Story of Hypnotism*, New York, Prentice Hall.

Maynard, James (1989). *Transpersonal Hypnotherapy*, Seattle, WA, Transpersonal Press.

McGill, Ormond (1979). *Hypnotism and Mysticism of India*, Los Angeles, Westwood Publishing Co.

McGill, Ormond (1977). *Professional Stage Hypnotism*, Glenndale, CA, Westwood Publishing Co.

McGill, Ormond (1975). *The Art of Stage Hypnotism*, Alhambra, CA, Borden Publishing.

Merloo, Joost (1956). *Mental Seduction and Menticide*, London, Jonathan Cape.

Moine, Donald & Kenneth Lloyd (1990). *Unlimited Selling Power*, Engelwood Cliffs, NJ, Prentice Hall.

Moll, Albert (1890). *Hypnotism* (2 vols), New York, Scribner & Welford (Reprinted by De Capo Press International, 1982).

Moore, George Foot (1914). *Metem-Psychosis*, Cambridge, Mass., Harvard University Press.

Munro, Henry (1907). *A Handbook of Suggestive Therapeutics*, Applied Hypnotism, Psychic Science, St. Louis, C.V. Mosby Publishing Co.

Neal & Clark eds. (1900). *Hypnotism and Hypnotic Suggestion*, New York, Rochester 1900 (Reprinted by Lindsay, Bradley, IL, 1987; Health Research, 1996).

Orton, Lewis (1948). *Hypnotism Made Practical* (2 vols), London, Thorsons.

Ousby, William J. (1966). *The Theory and Practice of Hypnotism*, London, Thorsons.

Pavlov, I.P. (1927, 1960). *Conditioned Reflexes*, New York, Dover Publications.

Pearson, (1790). *A Plain and Rational Account of the Nature & Effect of Animal Magnetism*, London, W. & J. Strafford.

Peiffer, Vera (1996). *Principles of Hypnotherapy*, London, Thorsons.

Petrie, Sidney & R. Stone (1968). *What Modern Hypnotism Can Do For You*, New York, Hawthorn Books Inc.

Powers, Melvin (1953). *Advanced Techniques of Hypnosis*, Los Angeles, Wilshire Press.

Powers, Melvin (1961). *A Practical Guide to Self Hypnosis*, Los Angeles, Wilshire Press.

Powers, Melvin (1949). *Hypnotism Revealed*, Los Angeles, Wilshire Press.

Powers, Melvin (1956, 1979). *Self Hypnosis*, Los Angeles, Wilshire Press.

Quackenbos, John Duncan (1901). *Hypnotism in Mental and Moral Culture*, New York, Harper & Bros.

Quimby, Phinneas Parkhurst (Horatio W. Dresser ed.) (1921, 1961). *The Quimby Manuscripts*, Secaucus, NJ, Citadel Press.

Ramacharaka, Yogi. *The Science of Psychic Healing*, London, L.N. Fowler.

Randall, Frank H. (1897). *Practical Instruction in Mesmerism*, London, Roxburghe Press, Ltd.

Randall, Frank H. (1901). *Your Mesmeric Forces & How to Develop Them*, London, L.N. Fowler (Reprinted by Health Research, 1996).

Rhodes, Raphael (1950). *Hypnosis: Theory Practice and Appplication*, Secaucus, NJ, Citadel Press.

Rhodes, Raphael ed. (1957). *Therapy Through Hypnosis*, Secaucus, NJ, Citadel Press.

Root-Bernstein, Robert (1993). *Rethinking AIDS, The Tragic Cost of Premature Consensus*, New York, MacMillan.

Rossi, Ernest (1980). *The Collected Papers of Milton H. Erickson*, New York, Irvington Publishers.

Rossi, Ernest (1986). *The Psychobiology of Mind/Body Healing*, New York, W.W. Norton.

Rossi, Ernest (1991). *The 20-Minute Break*, Los Angeles, CA, Jeremy P. Tarcher, Inc.

Rossi, Ernest & David Cheek (1988). *Mind Body Therapy*, New York, W.W. Norton.

Sage, X. LaMotte (1897,1901). *Hypnotism as it Is*, Rochester, NY, New York State Publishing Company.

Salter, Andrew (1949). *Conditioned Reflex Therapy*, Creative Age Press.

Salter, Andrew (1944). *What is Hypnosis?* (2 vols), Secaucus, NJ, Citadel Press.

Santanelli (James H. Loryea) (1902, 1980). *The Law of Suggestion*, Columbus, OH, Pyramid Press.

Satow, Louis (1923). *Hypnotism and Suggestion*, London, George Allen & Unwin.

Scheflin, Alan & Jerold Shapiro (1989). *Trance on Trial*, New York, Guilford Press.

Schofield, Alfred (1899). *The Unconscious Mind*, London, Hodder & Stoughton.

Shaftesbury, Edmund (1931). *Advanced Magnetism*, Meriden, Conn., Ralston University Press.

Shaftesbury, Edmund (1928). *Be Your Own Doctor*, Meriden, Conn., Ralston University Press.

Shaftesbury, Edmund (1926). *Instantaneous Personal Magnetism*, Meriden, Conn., Ralston University Press, (Reprinted by Kessinger Publishing Co., 1998).

Shaftesbury, Edmund (1936). *Life's Secrets Revealed*, Meriden, Conn., Ralston University Press.

Shaftesbury, Edmund (1931). *Mental Magnetism*, Meriden, Conn., Ralston University Press (Reprinted by Kessinger Publishing Co., 1996).

Shaftesbury, Edmund (1929). *Operations of the Other Mind*, Meriden, Conn., Ralston University Press.

Shaftesbury, Edmund (1932). *The Great Psychic: The Master Mind*, Meriden, Conn., Ralston University Press.

Shaftesbury, Edmund (1896). *Transference of Thought*, Meriden, Conn., Ralston University Press.

Shrader, Wesley (1969). *The Amazing Power of Hypnosis*, New York, Barnes & Noble.

Shreeve, Caroline & David Shreeve (1984). *The Healing Power of Hypnotism*, London, Thorsons.

Sidis, Boris (Introduction by W. James) (1898). *The Psychology of Suggestion*, New York, D. Appleton & Co.

Sinett, A.P. (1892). *The Rationale of Mesmerism*, London, Kegan, Paul & Trench.

Sparks, Laurence (1962). *Self Hypnosis: A Conditioned Reflex*, Los Angeles, Wilshire Press.

Spiegel, David & Herbert Spiegel (1978). *Trance and Treatment*, New York, Basic Books.

Stone, Robert B. (1976). *The Power of Miracle Metaphysics*, West Nyack, NY, Parker Publishing.

Sturt, Mary (1925). *The Psychology of Time*, London, Kegan, Paul, Trench, Trubner & Co.

Tebbetts, Charles (1988). *Self Hypnosis & Other Mind-Expanding Techniques*, Rocklin, CA, Prima Publishing.

Teitelbaum, Hyram (1965). *Hypnosis Induction Techniques*, Springfield, IL, Charles C. Thomas.

Teste, Alphonse (1843). *A Practical Manual of Animal Magnetism*, London, H. Balliere.

Townshend, Chauncy Hare (1854). *Mesmerism Proved True*, London, Thomas Bosworth.

Tracey, David F. (1954). *How to Use Hypnosis*, (2 vols), London, Arco Publishing Co. Ltd.

Tracey, David F. (1952). *Hypnosis*, New York, Sterling Publishers.

Tucke, D. Hack, 1884. *Sleep Walking and Hypnotism*, London, J.A. Churchill.

Tuckey, Lloyd (1889, 1892). *Psycho-Therapeutics or Treatment by Hypnotism and Suggestion*, New York, G.P. Putnam's Sons; London, Bailliere, Tindall & Cox.

Van Pelt, S.J. (1950). *Hypnotism and The Power Within*, New York, Skeffington & Son Ltd.

Van Pelt, S.J. (1958). *Secrets of Hypnotism*, London, Neville Spearman.

Van Pelt, S.J., G. Ambrose & G. Newbold (1957). *Medical Hypnosis Handbook*, Hollywood, CA, Wilshire Press.

Van Vogt, A.E. & C.E. Cooke (1965). *The Hypnotism Handbook*, Alhambra, CA, Borden Publishing.

Verner, Alexander (1910). *Medical Hypnotism and Suggestion*, Chicago, IL, Yogi Publication Society.

Von Reichenbach, Baron (1852). *The Od Force*, New England, Hobart & Robbins (Reprinted by Kessinger Publishing Co., 1996).

Warman, Edward (1910). *Psychic Science Series-Hypnotism*, London, A.C. McClurg & Co.

Watkins, John (1986). *Hypnotherapeutic Techniques*, New York, Irvington Publishers.

Weitzenhoffer, Andre M. (1957). *General Techniques of Hypnotism*, New York, Grune & Stratton.

Weitzenhoffer, Andre (1989). *The Practice of Hypnotism* (2 vols), New York, John Wiley & Sons.

Whipple, Leander Edmund (1893, 1907). *Mental Healing*, New York, The Metaphysical Publishing Company.

Wingfield, Hugh E. (1920). *An Introduction to Hypnotism*, London, Bailliere, Tindall & Cox.

Winn, Ralph (1939, 1956). *Hypnotism Made Easy*, Los Angeles, Wilshire Press.

Wolberg, Lewis (1948). *Medical Hypnosis* (2 vols), New York, Grune & Stratton.

Wyckoff, James (1975). *Franz Anton Mesmer, Between God and Devil*, Engelwood Cliffs, NJ, Prentice Hall.

Wynn, Ralph (1939, 1956, 1960). *Scientific Hypnotism*, Los Angeles, Wilshire Press.

Young, L.E. (1899). *The Science of Hypnotism: The Wonder of the 20th Century*, Baltimore, I & M Ottenheimer.

Zeig, Jeffrey (1980). *A Teaching Seminar with Milton H. Erickson*, New York, Brunner Mazel.

Zeig, Jeffrey & S. Lankton eds. (1988). *Developing Ericksonian Therapy*, New York, Brunner Mazel.

Zeig, Jeffrey (1985). *Experiencing Erickson*, New York, Brunner Mazel.

Zweig, Stefan (1932, 1962). *Mental Healers*, New York, Viking Press.

Index

A

'ABCD' signal   112
Achieveable Outcome   45
actualizing   21, 22, 66, 136, 145, 146
ad-lib   91
Adler, Alfred   14
Advanced Neuro Dynamics   107, 175
age regression   132
allopathic   6
ambiguity   29, 33, 73, 109, 115
      phonological   33
      syntactic   33
ambiguous language   25, 29
American Pacific University   175
American Institute of Hypnotherapy   95, 126
amnesia   21, 62-63, 130, 146
amnesia for suggestions   21
analgesia   62, 64
anchor   95
anesthesia   62, 64-65
      glove   62, 64
anesthetic   13, 64-65
Animal Magnetism   12
The Answer Within   126
arm levitation   75, 86, 91, 136, 180
associations   71
attention   4, 24, 37-38, 44, 48, 70-71, 76, 83, 85-86, 112, 115-117, 120, 122-123, 148, 157, 167-168
automatic movement   62, 64, 132, 183

B

back pain   186-89
behaviour   6, 19, 22, 39-40, 65, 70, 79, 83, 86, 96, 99, 112, 147, 157, 182

D

N

O

P

Q

R

S

trigger   72, 142, 147, 173
truisms   74-75
trust   53, 110, 154, 176
twentieth century   5, 14, 15
Twitmeyer, William   14-15

U

Unconscious Mind   3-6, 11, 16, 19-20, 22-23, 25, 29, 38-39, 44, 48,
        51, 53, 56, 71-78, 85, 90, 96-102, 105-107, 109-112, 115-117,
        120-122, 124, 126, 135-137, 141, 143-148, 152, 168-169, 173-
        174, 176, 182, 186, 188
Unconscious   3-7, 11, 16, 19-23, 25, 29, 33, 38-39, 44, 48, 51, 53,
        56, 61, 66, 71-78, 84-85, 88-91, 95-102, 105-107, 109-112,
        115-118, 120-124, 126, 133, 135-137, 141, 143-148, 152, 168-
        169, 173-174, 176, 179, 181, 182, 185-186, 188
underlying cause   105
Universal Quantifier   31, 46
Unspecified Comparison   32
Unspecified Predicate   31
utilization   3, 34-35, 37-40, 51, 61, 70, 79, 96, 115-116, 137, 142,
        182
Utilization Exercise   39, 51
utilization approach   70, 79

V

values   52, 64, 71, 95
verbs   31, 47
Vienna   11-12
Visual Hallucinations   134, 186, 188
voice   29, 56, 73, 83, 86, 90, 117, 131, 133, 146, 168, 183, 185
        tone   73, 83, 86, 117

W

weak legs   132, 184
weight loss   73

Ericksonian Approaches
A Comprehensive Manual
Rubin Battino MS & Thomas L. South PhD

Already highly acclaimed, this is an outstanding training manual in the art of Ericksonian hypnotherapy. Designed to be easily accessible, it provides a systematic approach to learning set against a clinical background, developing the reader's learning over twenty-two chapters that include the history of hypnosis, myths and misconceptions, rapport-building skills, language forms, basic and advanced inductions, utilisation of ideo-dynamic responses, basic and advanced metaphor, and Ericksonian approaches in medicine, dentistry, substance abuse and life-threatening diseases.

Also available: a companion audiotape – ISBN 189983642X 65 mins.

"This book should undoubtedly be read and re-read by any who consider themselves to be hypnotherapists. But it should not be limited to them. If people who are not interested in the subject of hypnotherapy are not drawn to it, this will be a loss for anyone who uses language in the course of therapeutic work…. I highly recommend this book."
– Barry Winbolt, *The New Therapist*.

Rubin Battino MS has a private practice in Yellow Springs, Ohio. He teaches courses periodically for the Department of Human Resources at Wright State University where he holds the rank of adjunct professor. He has over six years of experience as a facilitator in a Bernie Siegel style support group for people who have life-threatening diseases and those who support them. He is President of the Milton H. Erickson Society of Dayton, co-chair of an ad hoc committee to establish certification standards for training in Ericksonian hypnotherapy for the societies and institutes affiliated with the Milton H. Erickson Foundation. He has developed and teaches courses in Ericksonian hypnotherapy at Wright State University with T.L. South. He is Professor Emeritus of chemistry.

Thomas L. South PhD has his doctorate in clinical psychology from the Union Institute. He has conducted workshops for the Associate Trainers in Clinical Hypnosis, and has developed and taught courses in Ericksonian approaches at the University of Dayton and with Rubin Battino at Wright State University. He invited the faculty at the Third International Congress on Ericksonian Approaches to Hypnosis and Psychotherapy. He is the author of a chapter entitled "Hypnosis in Childbirth: A Case Study in Anesthesia." Dr. South is the founder and first president of the Milton H. Erickson Society of Dayton, and is presently a staff psychologist at the Twin Valley Psychiatric System – Dayton Forensic Unit. He has had a private practice for many years.

HARDBACK   564 PAGES   ISBN: 1899836314

Now available in paperback

Scripts And Strategies In Hypnotherapy
Roger P. Allen

The use of scripts in induction procedures provides a framework upon which to build successful therapy sessions. Written by a practising hypnotherapist, this is a rich, comprehensive source of scripts and strategies to be used by hypnotherapists of all levels of experience. Areas covered include inductions, deepeners and actual scripts for a wide range of problems, from nail biting to getting a good night's sleep, sports performance to past-life recall, pain management to resolving sexual problems. All scripts may be used as they stand or adapted for specific situations. A runaway bestseller.

"Imaginative, practical and essential for anyone getting started in hypnotherapy."
– Martin Roberts PhD, author of *Change Management Excellence*.

PAPERBACK   180 PAGES   ISBN: 1899836462

Orders to:

The Anglo American Book Company Ltd.

FREEPOST SS1340,
Crown Buildings, Bancyfelin, Carmarthen, Wales SA33 4ZZ
Tel: 01267 211880/211886 Fax: 01267 211882
(Lines open 9am – 5.30pm Mon – Fri)

E-mail address: books@anglo-american.co.uk

Web site: anglo-american.co.uk

Or visit the
Crown House Publishing Web site at:

w w w . c r o w n h o u s e . c o . u k